McGraw-Hill's Concise
Guide to Writing
Research Papers

McGraw-Hill's Concise Guide to Writing Research Papers

Carol Ellison

New York Chicago San Francisco Lisbon
London Madrid Mexico City Milan New Delhi
San Juan Seoul Singapore Sydney Toronto

The McGraw·Hill Companies

Copyright © 2010 by The McGraw-Hill Companies. All rights reserved. Printed in the United States of America. Except as permitted under the United States Copyright Act of 1976, no part of this publication may be reproduced or distributed in any form or by any means, or stored in a database or retrieval system, without the prior written permission of the publisher.

1 2 3 4 5 6 7 8 9 0   WFR/WFR   0 1 0

ISBN: 978-0-07-162989-8
MHID: 0-07-162989-0

This book is printed on acid-free paper.

McGraw-Hill books are available at special quantity discounts to use as premiums and sales promotions, or for use in corporate training programs. To contact a representative please e-mail us at bulksales@mcgraw-hill.com.

This publication is designed to provide accurate and authoritative information in regard to the subject matter covered. It is sold with the understanding that neither the author nor the publisher is engaged in rendering legal, accounting, or other professional services. If legal advice or other expert assistance is required, the services of a competent professional person should be sought.

—*From a Declaration of Principles jointly adopted by a committee of the American Bar Association and a Committee of Publishers.*

The Library of Congress Cataloging-in-Publication Data

Ellison, Carol.
  McGraw-Hill's concise guide to writing research papers / by Carol Ellison.
      p. cm.
Includes bibliographical references.
ISBN-13: 978-0-07-162989-8
ISBN-10: 0-07-162989-0
  1. Report writing–Handbooks, manuals, etc. 2. Research–Handbooks, manuals, etc. I. Title. II. Title: Concise guide to writing research papers.

LB2369.E35 2010

808'.042--dc22   2009045535

Contents

Contents

Contents

Preface

What is a "perfect" research paper? For students, the perfect research paper is the one that earns an A, wins an academic competition, or earns them a scholarly award. For others tasked with writing research papers, the "perfect" paper may be one that earns them a raise or promotion or recognition within their company or the industry in which they work.

The strategies and tips in this book are written primarily for students at the high school and university level. However, they will be helpful to anyone who is confronted with the task of writing a research paper and is looking for help.

The good news here is that anyone can learn to write a research paper. You do not need to be a "born writer." Unlike creative writing where quality is largely a function of imagination, the expository writing done for research papers is based on standard formats, expectations, and stylistic guidelines that anyone can follow.

Still, writing an effective research paper can be a daunting task. While a research paper does not rely heavily on the writer's inspiration, it does require persistence, attention to detail, and a willingness to read, revise, and perfect what was written—many times if necessary. But is that so very different from any other

Preface

skill that is important in our lives? Remember falling again and again until you learned to ride a two-wheel bike, missing the ball over and over until you learned to bat, or making the most horrendous noises on the piano until you properly struck a chord? Expository writing is a lot like that. We learn by doing, and we get better with practice. Improvement depends upon the guidance we get along the way. This book is designed to deliver that.

McGraw-Hill's Concise
Guide to Writing
Research Papers

Chapter 1

Getting Started

Research papers begin with a writing assignment. It may be specific. It may be general. It may assign you a topic and point you in the direction the research should take. Or it may offer a great deal of flexibility, allowing you to pick your topic and stage your own investigation. It serves as a roadmap to what you must do. It is your first clue to what your instructor expects of you. If you have a thorough understanding of what is expected of you, you will be better able to deliver it.

Tackling a research project is, in many ways, like preparing to run a race. You have no hope of finishing among the leaders if you have no idea where the finishing line is or how to get there. That may sound sophomoric but the vast majority of research projects that end in failure do so because the writer proceeded with no clear idea of what was expected and delivered something off the mark.

The first step you take in tackling the paper should point you in the direction of a successful finish. You need to know what is expected of you and how to prepare to deliver it. By understanding where you need to end up, you will spare yourself a lot of trial and error in getting there.

First Steps

- Identify the expectations (due date, length, etc.).
- Interpret the assignment.
- Analyze the audience.
- Choose a topic.
- Write a working thesis.
- Write a proposal.

Interpreting the Assignment

Knowing precisely what you need to produce is the first step to producing a perfect paper. Not only will it spare you the frustration of assembling material that may not be appropriate to the assignment, but it will assure you of a better grade. One of the first questions on an instructor's mind is: *Did this student understand the assignment?* A student's ability to deliver what the assignment requests shows the teacher or professor that the student possesses the skills to properly interpret instructions and identify expectations.

Research papers typically begin with an assignment that identifies your teacher's expectations and provides the information you need to know to complete the assignment.

What You Should Know before You Start

- What is the purpose of the assignment? What does your instructor expect you to learn?
- Is there an assigned topic? Can you choose your own?
- What kinds of sources should you use?
- How many sources should you use?

- Are print and online sources equally acceptable?
- When is the paper due?
- How long should it be?
- How should the paper be formatted?
- How should bibliographic information be presented?
- What are the qualities of a paper that gets an A, B, C, or D?

You cannot produce a perfect paper if you do not know what "perfection" means to your teacher or the person who will be reading and evaluating it. More important than the basic expectations are those that actually tell you what to do. Assignments are often worded very deliberately to test how well students read, interpret, and respond to the expectations that are outlined. Your instructor may want to know how well you can summarize new ideas and complex material, for instance, or whether you can present a logical argument to support an opinion or advocate an idea. Another assignment might spell out how you should conduct your research by specifying the types of sources you should consult. Others may use words like *analyze, discuss,* or *investigate* to describe what is expected. Do not take these words lightly. They have specific meanings. Learn to recognize the learning goals in an assignment.

When you receive an assignment, read it thoroughly and be prepared to ask your instructor about anything that is unclear to you. Make a list of the stated expectations. True, you already have these on the assignment sheet but writing them down will emphasize them in your mind and help you to remember them. If you receive the criteria for how your paper will be graded, examine them as closely as you do the assignment to determine what you must do to achieve the grade you want. If your teacher does not provide the grading criteria, ask what they are. An example of grading criteria that we use for writing composition classes at Rutgers University Newark campus appears below:

Grade Criteria

Grade of A: An essay that merits an A demonstrates a generally high degree of competence and control of language. Typically, such an essay meets all of the following criteria:

- Responds to the assignment thoroughly, thoughtfully, and with insight or originality.
- Demonstrates strong reading comprehension of the assigned texts.
- Is well-developed and supports analysis with effective textual evidence, reasons, examples, and details.
- Is well-focused and well-organized, demonstrating strong control over the conventions of analytical writing.
- Demonstrates facility with language, using effective vocabulary and sentence variety.
- Demonstrates strong control of grammar, the rules of usage, and mechanics of standard English but may have minor errors.

Grade of B: An essay that receives a B is written in a clearly competent manner and displays generally consistent control of language. Typically, such an essay meets all of the following criteria:

Getting Started

- Responds to all elements of the assignment competently and thoughtfully.
- Demonstrates an adequate understanding of the readings.
- Is adequately developed, using appropriate textual evidences, reasons, examples, and details.
- Is focused and effectively organized, demonstrating control of the conventions of analytical essay writing.
- Demonstrates strong language competence and uses appropriate vocabulary and sentence variety.
- Shows good control of grammar, the rules of usage, and mechanics of standard English, although it may have some errors and minor lapses in quality.

Grade of C: An essay that earns a grade of C demonstrates some competence but is limited in one or more of the following ways:

- Does not address all parts of the writing assignment.
- Does not demonstrate an adequate understanding of the readings.
- Is thinly developed, often relying on assertions with little textual evidence or few relevant reasons, examples, and details.
- Is adequately focused and/or adequately organized, but connections between the parts could be more explicit.
- Demonstrates limited facility with language and minimal sentence variety.
- Demonstrates inconsistent control of grammar, usage, and the mechanics of writing.

Grade of D: An essay receives a grade of D if it has one or more of the following flaws:

- Is unclear and/or seriously limited in its response to the writing assignment.

- Demonstrates a limited reading or misreading of the texts.

- Is unfocused and/or disorganized, demonstrating little control of the conventions of analytical essay writing.

- Demonstrates serious errors in the use of language, which may interfere with meaning.

- Demonstrates serious errors in grammar, usage, and mechanics, which may interfere with meaning.

Grade of F: An essay receives a grade of F when it:

- Demonstrates little or no ability to develop an organized response to the writing assignment.

- Contains severe writing errors that persistently obscure meaning.

Make note of any specific information or ideas that the assignment asks you to discuss. It helps to raise your hand, ask any questions you may have, and take notes. Any information you receive will help you in your pursuit of the "perfect" paper.

Make every effort to ensure that you understand what your instructor is requesting. That way, you know what to deliver.

Types of Assignments

Writing assignments are not created equal. The approach you take to receive an A in an assignment for one class will not necessary work well for you in another. You should expect that any writing assignment, whether it is given at the high school or college level, will differ according to the class you are taking and expectations your instructor outlines for the class. Even within a class, an instructor's expectations are likely to change from assignment to assignment. Getting a good grade is not a function of "psyching out" your instructor. It is a function of understanding the assignment and what you are being asked to do.

The High School Level

In high school, research papers are generally assigned to test a student's ability to look up information and explain it adequately in his or her own words. Here is a list of the kinds of assignments typically given in high school and what they mean:

- *Summary:* An abbreviated account of a larger article, book, or other work.
  Examples: Book report, movie review, or a summary of something you read in the news or saw on TV.
- *Description:* A detailed account of what things look like. Descriptions that help readers "see" what you are talking about are especially useful to clarify events, conditions, or concepts that might be unfamiliar to the reader. Good descriptions make appropriate use of adjectives and adverbs, metaphors, similes, and examples to build readers' understanding.

Examples: A history report about life in another time or a geography report about the culture and industries in another country.

■ *Explanation:* A description that tells why certain conditions exist or certain events occur. Explanations attempt to identify the cause or causes that create an effect. They attempt to answer the question, "Why"?

Examples: A science report.

■ *Process:* A description of conditions that must exist and actions that must be taken to produce an outcome.

Examples: Instructions someone should follow to do something successfully, such as following the steps in an experiment, or directions to a destination.

■ *Narrative:* A story about something that happened. Narratives are often told in chronological order with a beginning, middle, and end.

Examples: "What I Did on My Summer Vacation"

The University Level

At the university, a great deal more is expected. Assignments become more complex. Instead of simply asking you to summarize or describe something, the assignment typically will present you with a challenge. Often, too, the assignment is not even called an "assignment." Instead, it is called a "writing prompt," meaning that the purpose of the assignment is to "prompt" your thinking and elicit a thorough written response from you. Writing prompts usually call upon the writer to use a combination of the approaches learned in high school (those listed above), as well as employ other approaches and strategies to advance new ideas, opinions, and arguments about the topic under discussion.

The path to producing a perfect paper begins with understanding what those goals are and how to identify them in the assignment. Below is a list of terms that professors often use in writing prompts and what they mean:

- *Analyze* relationships among facts, trends, theories, and issues. Point out their significant likes and differences and tell why they are meaningful.
- *Argue* in defense of (or against) a concept, opinion, position, thesis, or point of view. Strong arguments apply logic and point out fallacies, errors, and "fuzzy" thinking.
- *Categorize* or *classify* items, concepts, or events by sorting them in sets of predefined qualities or conditions according to their similarities.
- *Compare and contrast* two or more events, ideas, or opinions by identifying their similarities and/or differences. (Look for similarities when you compare two things; look for differences when you contrast them.)
- *Define* the meaning of an unfamiliar term, phrase, or concept by describing the concept behind it.
- *Discuss* the implications of your research or various points of view on your topic by looking at different sides of the issue and pointing out their merits.
- *Examine* a topic in minute detail by describing it as if it were under a microscope.
- *Illustrate* a concept by using many significant details to describe it.

- *Interpret* a set of facts or events by explaining their significance and importance to your reader, or to other audiences with other needs or interests.

- *Give your opinion* by telling what you think about the topic and provide an explanation about why you think it.

- *Reason* (the verb, not the noun) by presenting the logical thought process required to support a specific conclusion.

- *Synthesize* information from a variety of sources to support a single thesis, opinion, or conclusion.

- *Theorize* by presenting your own hypothesis, or best guess, about why things are the way they are.

Choosing a Research Topic

Topics for some research papers will be assigned to you, along with very specific requirements that you must follow in completing the paper. Others allow you to choose the topic you will research.

Many assignments are deliberately open-ended, allowing students to pick their own topics and pursue their own research. If your assignment is open-ended, you will have lots of latitude to research a topic that interests you, based on whatever guidelines or parameters your instructor specifies. The challenge then becomes finding a topic and devising a thesis and arguments to support it.

Below is an example of an open-ended writing assignment from a freshman composition course. It is designed to determine how effectively students can identify and control a topic, construct their own thesis, find appropriate research to support the thesis, and use that research to present arguments their audience would find convincing.

Example assignment:

Pick an issue that interests you and find at least three newspaper articles or editorials from different sources that express differing points of view on the issue. Produce a five-page paper, including four pages plus a Works Cited page, that analyzes the various points of view. What appears to be the best course of action, based on the merits of the arguments that the articles present? Be sure to use arguments from each of your sources as you explore the issue. Paraphrase, summarize, and quote them accurately and be sure to cite them according to MLA style.

Open-ended assignments can be fun. They allow you to pursue your own interests but they can also be frustrating because they require you to make decisions that specific assignments make for you. Students often lament, "I don't know what to write about," or they spend a great deal of time gathering research on vague topics that do not address their thesis.

The job becomes much easier if you have a topic, one that is specific and focused and offers something to say. Coming up with one is the challenge but it is not as difficult as it sounds.

Most of us know more—a lot more—than we think we know about the world around us and the subjects we study in school. At a minimum, we all hold opinions about what is happening in our world, and, whether we realize it or not, we formed those opinions based on information and experience we gathered somewhere in life. If you find yourself stuck for a topic, ask yourself a few questions to get your creative juices flowing. You will find you have a lot more to say about topics that you are involved with or that pique your interest than topics others might suggest.

Here are some things to consider when choosing a research topic:

- Your hobbies and special interests.
- Class discussions that caught your attention and aroused your interest.
- Things you have read that caught your attention and aroused your interest.
- True stories you have heard about on the radio or saw on TV that provoked a reaction from you and made you happy, sad, angry, or disgusted.
- Things you have overheard that you would like to know more about.
- Your hopes for the future.
- Your worries about the future.
- Things you dream about.
- Issues you think someone should do something about.

Make a list of everything that comes to mind. You can use this list to begin brainstorming. Behind each topic, write a sentence or two about why it interests you. Do not correct or edit what you have written. Just write whatever comes to you.

When you have finished the list, pick the topic that most interests you—one that you actually *want* to write about and that you feel you would have a lot to say about. Open-ended research papers tend to be large, even massive, projects. They are often assigned weeks ahead of when they are due in order to give you plenty of time to find material to support your arguments. Since you are going to be living with the topic for a while, it might as well be something you care about.

After you have picked a topic, begin to focus it by writing down anything you can think about the topic you chose. Things to consider as you narrow your topic:

- Your opinion about it.
- Interesting things you have heard about it.
- Things you have read about it.
- Others' observations on it.
- Any facts, assumptions, rumors, myths, and even the misimpressions and false representations you have heard about it.

If you are assigned a research topic, you do not have a lot of flexibility. The assignment that appears below is from a college freshman-level composition course. It requires students to refer to the readings assigned in class, develop a central idea (or thesis), and find arguments to support it. Assignments such as this are designed to determine how well students understand certain readings and how well they can represent their understanding to others.

Example assignment:

The ability of music to help people rise above difficult circumstances is a key theme in Oliver Sacks' book, *Musicophilia*. Discuss how that affects the lives and mindsets of the two main characters in James Baldwin's short story, "Sonny's Blues."

If the assignment requires you to write about a specific topic, write about it. A word to the wise is important here. Never stray from an assignment and head off in a direction all your own unless you first get approval from your instructor.

One of the best ways to ensure a less-than-perfect grade is to research a topic that in no way resembles the one you were assigned. No matter how brilliant your research or how lovely your prose, you will most likely receive an F if you fail to deliver what the assignment requests.

As noted earlier, instructors usually construct assignments with learning goals in mind. A student's failure to correctly respond to an assignment means that he or she has not met those goals. Worse, it raises a red flag to the instructor who may question whether the student understood the assignment or, worse, whether the student got lazy and desperate and found a well-written essay on the Internet and decided to submit it instead.

If you want to investigate a topic that was not assigned, ask your instructor if you can. Often, an instructor will be happy to let you follow your passion and conduct your own research, but always ask permission before you do.

Developing a Working Thesis

A thesis is a claim that you intend to prove using sound, well-reasoned arguments drawn from careful research. It will be the central statement in your paper when you actually sit down to write. In all likelihood, your working thesis will not be the one that you actually present in your paper.

A working thesis simply aims to get you started on your research. You need it as an idea to guide you. Writing instructors often refer to this process of developing an idea into a working thesis as "invention." You are "inventing" ideas for your paper. When you have finished this invention stage, you will find that you have the basis for a thesis and a good sense of direction in identifying the research you will need to support it.

The working thesis should be aimed at helping you narrow and manage your topic. A working thesis that is phrased in the form of a question can help guide your research. A good working thesis makes the job more manageable. Keep it focused. Avoid making it too general. Theses that are too general often ramble and result in papers that lose focus and therefore earn low grades.

Here are some examples of questions for working theses that are general and not well focused:

- Should more money be spent on education?
- How can the government balance the budget?
- Why should we study art?
- What should we do about global warming?
- How can we eliminate poverty?
- How should we respond to the energy crisis?

The following examples, however, are focused on specific issues that can be more easily researched:

- Should more government-backed student loans be made available?
- Should cuts in military spending be enacted before cutting domestic spending to balance the national budget?
- Should the study of art history or the creative arts receive greater emphasis in America's high schools?
- Is wind energy a viable alternative to fossil fuels?
- Will the extension of unemployment benefits improve life for the nation's unemployed?

- Will the sale of electric vehicles reduce American dependence on foreign oil?

Analyzing Your Audience

A key test of a perfect paper is how well it resonates with its audience. It is useful, before you begin, to create a profile of a theoretical reader.

Rather than focus on your instructor as your audience, assume you are addressing intelligent people of approximately the same age and educational level as yourself. Assume that they have not yet read the material you have read and that you will need to provide sufficient background to ensure that the audience will understand and accept your arguments. You will determine how to present your information and ideas according to the impact you hope they will have on the reader.

What You Should Know about Members of Your Audience

- Approximate age.
- Approximate educational level.
- Experiences they have in common.
- Why they would be interested in your topic.
- How much the average reader should already know about your topic.
- What questions a reader is likely to have.
- How that reader might react to your arguments.

Writing a Proposal

Research proposals are only occasionally required in high school courses, sometimes in freshman-level college courses, and often in upper-level college business and science courses. However, even if your research assignment does not require you to submit a proposal, it is a good idea to develop one for your own purposes. A proposal helps you to organize ideas that can guide the research process. Proposals allow you to start the thought process needed to focus your ideas. A good research proposal will identify the topic, present a working thesis, and offer a plan to prove it.

Think of your proposal as an outline for how you will pursue your research and structure your paper.

Your proposal should:

- Identify your topic.
- Present a working thesis.
- Identify how you will conduct your research.
- Present a hypothesis for what you expect to prove.

Chapter 2

Doing Your Research

The Internet, with its speed and ubiquity, has made research much easier than it once was. Thanks to the Internet, you have a library of millions of sources at your disposal 24 hours a day.

This abundance of research, however, can be overwhelming. Today the problem is not how to find research material but how to work your way through the thousands (or even millions) of documents that turn up in your search. Enter a search word or phrase about a topic, any topic, into Google, Yahoo, or whatever your favorite search engine might be, and in seconds you will be presented with pages upon pages of two-line summaries of articles that contain it. Google and other search engines "weight" the results by putting the most likely matches at the top, but the chore of finding the perfect source to meet your research needs is still left to you.

Useful Research Sites and Search Engines

Topic	Search site
Academic	ReferenceDesk.org (www.referencedesk.org)
	Librarians' Internet Index (http://lii.org)
	Google Scholar (http://scholar.google.com)
	Merriam-Webster Dictionary (www.merriam-webster.com/)
Business	bNet (www.bnet.com)
	Harvard Business Review (www.hbr.org)
Government	Firstgov.gov (www.usa.gov/Topics/Teens.shtml)
	Searchgov.com (www.searchgov.com)
News	Google News (http://news.google.com)
	Newspaper Archive (www.newspaperarchive.com)
Science	Scirus (www.scirus.com)

Searching the Internet

Google is, no doubt, the most used and, certainly, the best-known search engine on the Internet. The question for researchers who use it and other search engines that scan the entire Internet is: How reliable is the information?

One thing you need to know when you do Internet research is that anyone can publish anything on the Web. For that reason, it can be very difficult to determine if the articles you find are based on complete, factual, and reliable information. It is not always easy to determine whether the article you are reading makes conclusions based on facts or on other factors, such as advertising or promotion, that account for it being on the Web. E-commerce sites, for instance, are in the business of selling products. Political sites are in the business of selling ideas. The information on them may be what you are looking for but it may also be slanted to promote a particular product, agenda, or point of view. Search engines, such as Google, will find what you are looking for but they cannot evaluate the material to ensure it is acceptable for a research paper.

Google offers a number of specialized look-up features that help you control the search. Google Scholar (http://scholar. google.com), for instance, offers you a quick way to search across many different academic sources, including scholarly articles from academic journals and publishers, professional societies, and university Web sites. Google News (http://news. google.com) provides access to 25,000 news sources. Google Books (http://books.google.com) offers full-text searches of books, as well as related book reviews and other Web references to the books.

Utilizing Keyword Searches

Strategies for conducting a successful Internet search for sources differ according to whether you are accessing publications through the databases of an academic library or using a popular search engine, such as Google.

College students are encouraged to conduct their searches through their university's academic library. University search engines access catalogs of print sources, as well as print publications that are available in electronic format, including CDs, DVDs, and other multimedia resources that are available through the library network. They also provide access to electronic databases of publications that are available only to member libraries and research institutions.

Institutional search engines, such as those offered through your university, high school, or library system typically offer options for how to search for sources. These typically include quick look-ups under subject indexes, names of journals and databases, by authors and titles, and by keywords. This multiplicity of search mechanisms and the various resource catalogs and databases needed to access them can be confusing to newcomers. A few moments spent with a campus librarian who can orient you to the various search mechanisms can save you hours later.

Simple online look-ups can be useful when you do not have access to an academic library. Keywords describe your topic and can be combined in different ways to target and narrow your search. The search engine will look for those words throughout the text of many different articles and deliver a listing of the results in short summaries that can stretch on for pages. The search engine will find all references in the article and the words you are looking for may or may not be together. Using search operators, such as quotation marks around the exact phrase you want to find, and the words *and, or,* and *not,* can help you narrow the search and zero in on the articles that will be of greatest interest to you.

Phrases for Keyword Searches

- *Acronyms*: Use acronyms to find specific organizations, technologies, and scientific references.

  Examples: CDC (Centers for Disease Control)

  CDR (compact digital recorder)

  USC (University of Southern California)

- *Alternate spellings:* Use alternate and "sound-alike" spellings when you are unsure of names or the exact spelling of other terms.

  Examples: Gabriel LaBoiteaux, LaBoytoe, Labertew

- *Quotation marks (" "):* Use quotation marks to restrict your search to exact names and unique phrases inside the quotes.

  Examples: "Patrick Henry"

  "American Revolution"

  "Give me liberty or give me death"

- *And:* Use *and* to find articles that include both of the terms that it links.

  Example: "Patrick Henry" *and* "Give me liberty or give me death." This search will find only articles in which Patrick Henry's name and the full phrase, "Give me liberty or give me death," appear.

- *Or:* Use *or* to find articles that include one term or the other.

  Example: "Patrick Henry" *or* "Give me liberty or give me death." This search will find articles that mention Patrick Henry, articles that include the phrase, "Give me liberty or give me death," and articles that include both.

- *Not ... and not:* Use *not* or *and not* to deliberately exclude terms from your search.

  Example: "Patrick Henry" *not* "Give me liberty or give me death." This search will find articles that mention Patrick Henry but will exclude articles where his name appears with the phrase, "Give me liberty or give me death."

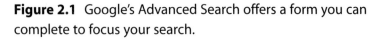

Figure 2.1 Google's Advanced Search offers a form you can complete to focus your search.

You can also control your search for information on the Internet by using the advanced search feature that is offered by many of the search engines. Advanced search essentially does what operators do, but, instead of entering the operators as part of your keyword search, you enter your search terms into a form. These forms can be very specific, even allowing you to restrict searches by the domain, number of finds you want returned on each page, and the time frame in which the material was posted to the Web. (See Figure 2.1.)

Using Library and Database Resources

Many times instructors will recommend, or even require, that student researchers avoid the popular search engines and, instead, take their search for information to the library. A visit to the library can transform your research efforts from simple look-ups into an educational experience that reveals many more resources that are open to you.

Not only is a library a source of countless texts, but it is also a place where you can seek the help of reference librarians who are schooled in using both print and digital resources to find reliable sources of information. Research librarians can also help you review and understand the requirements of an assignment, help you get started, and direct you in your search for information.

Libraries also offer you the advantage of being able to access books, articles, and other documents that are off-limits to average users. Databases such as Academic Search Premier, The Encyclopedia Britannica, EBSCO, ProQuest, and Lexis/Nexis offer access to a wide range of scholarly articles and journals that would otherwise require an ID and password for access. Most public and university libraries are members of these database networks, and they allow you to access them through computers in the library or by entering information from your library card or student ID. Many libraries offer their own search engines for finding articles in specialized databases. Usually, they allow you to search by categories (such as the humanities, science, or business) and click on a journal to browse it or to enter keywords to search across databases, much like you do when using an online search engine.

Finding Books at the Library

All libraries are repositories of recorded information, but not all libraries are alike. Their collections differ—both in the kinds of materials they offer and in how they categorize them. Public libraries, for instance, typically feature large sections of popular fiction, while research libraries may offer classical fiction but few titles that you would find on a current best-seller list. If you were looking for vampire novels, for instance, you are likely to find Bram Stoker's 1897 Gothic classic, *Dracula,* but do not expect it to share a shelf with the recent popular *Twilight* series by Stephanie Meyer.

Library collections are also limited by the physical capacity of the buildings. Fortunately, most of today's libraries are connected through networks to other, affiliated libraries, allowing you to order titles that can be delivered locally. The library's card catalog tells you what is in your library's collection and what can be ordered through its network.

All libraries use some form of cataloging or classification system to organize books. This allows library patrons to easily find the books on the shelves and tells librarians how to return them to their proper places when borrowers bring them back. Libraries use a variety of different classification schemes to index and shelve their books. The two most widely used are the Dewey Decimal Classification system (DDC) and the Library of Congress Classification system (LCC).

The Dewey Decimal Classification System (DDC) was developed by Melvil Dewey in 1876 to standardize the way in which books were organized within libraries. The Library of Congress Classification System (LCC) was developed in 1897 by the U.S. Library of Congress to meet the archival needs of the U.S. government. More than 95 percent of U.S. libraries use one or the other to provide a logical system for helping researchers and readers quickly locate titles about their topics. Most U.S. research and university libraries have moved to the LCC, while the DDC continues as the system most often found in public and school libraries. The categories in the two systems tend to reflect one another, although the precise alphanumeric system used by each is different. Both systems are constantly being expanded to keep up with the ever-growing body of published knowledge.

Researchers who lack a working knowledge of either system can always ask a librarian to point them in the right direction. However, it helps to have a basic understanding of how the systems work, particularly if you plan to browse the library shelves for books on your topic.

Decoding Call Numbers

Both the DDC and the LCC use alphanumeric systems to identify titles according to topic. Each title is assigned an identification number, called a "call number," according to how it is classified in the DDC or LCC.

Because it uses a system in which the categories and subcategories are divisible by 10, many researchers find DDC call numbers more logical and easier to use than the LCC's alphanumeric codes. The DDC organizes topics under 10 general categories that are identified by number. Each category is further divided into subcategories, also identified by number. DDC codes continue with a decimal-based system that is relatively easy to decipher as you zero in on your subject. Many times, the decimal is followed by a letter which indicates the first letter of the last name of the author.

The 10 general categories of the Dewey Decimal System include:

000	Generalities
100	Philosophy and psychology
200	Religion
300	Social sciences and anthropology
400	Language
500	Natural sciences and mathematics
600	Technology and applied sciences
700	The arts
800	Literature and rhetoric
900	Geography and history

For a list of the subclassifications under each category, see Appendix A in this book. For more information about the DDC, visit the Dewey Services page of the Online Computer Library Center, Inc. (OCLC) at www.oclc.org/dewey.

LCC call numbers begin with a letter, designating the general category, followed by either another letter or a number that designates the subcategory. Deciphering LCC codes is trickier and may require the help of a librarian. The first letter in an LCC call number refers to one of the 21 categories represented in the system. The initial digit is followed by a letter or number combination that represents the subcategory. However, some categories in the LCC (including E and F which represent the history of the Americas) use numbers to indicate the subcategory and others (such as D which represents some areas of history, and K which represents Law) use three letters. The digits that follow the category and subcategory in the call number further define the subject. The final three letter-number combination in the call number is called the "cutter number." It provides a code to the name of the author or the organization that sponsored the publication.

The 21 general categories of the LCC include:

A	General works
B	Philosophy, psychology, religion
C	Auxiliary sciences of history, such as archaeology and genealogy
D	World history and the history of Europe, Asia, Africa, Australia, New Zealand, and so on
E–F	History of the Americas
G	Geography, anthropology, recreation
H	Social sciences
J	Political science
K	Law
L	Education
M	Music and books on music
N	Fine arts
P	Language and literature
Q	Science
R	Medicine
S	Agriculture
T	Technology and engineering
U	Military science
V	Naval science
Z	Bibliography and library science, information resources

You will find a full list of LCC categories and subcategories in Appendix B of this book. More information about the LCC can be found online through the Library of Congress Cataloging Distribution Service at www.loc.gov/cds/classif.html.

Using Library Catalogs

No matter which system your library uses, your search for books at the library will begin with the library's catalog. A library catalog is much like any other catalog. It is a record of everything that is available to you. Items within the library are indexed by their call numbers and arranged on the shelves according to their categories and subcategories.

Using LCC and DDC Call Numbers

An example of how both systems work can be seen in Figure 2.2. The card, from the online catalog of the Public Library of Cincinnati and Hamilton County, which serves as a major regional research library, as well as the community lending library for southwest Ohio, uses both systems and displays call numbers for each in its catalog.

In this example, the card lists both the DDC and the LCC numbers for the book *Theodore Rex*, one volume in Edmund Morris' three-part biography of U.S. President Theodore Roosevelt.

The LCC call number is the top number circled on the screen. It is E757,M885 2001. The initial letter, E, indicates the category, history of the Americas. The subclass, history of the United States, is indicated by the number that follows (757). M885 is its cutter number. The cutter number begins with a letter to identify the first letter of the author's last name, M for Edmund Morris, and provides additional numeric references to identify the book. The number at the end, 2001, indicates the year of publication.

The Dewey Decimal call number, shown in the circle below the LCC, codes the number numerically according to a base–10 system in which the first number, in the hundreds column, represents the main category, and the second letter,

Figure 2.2 The online catalog of the Public Library of Cincinnati and Hamilton County uses both the DDC and LCC classification systems.

in the tens column, represents the subcategory. Unlike the LCC, there are no exceptions to this from category to category. The DCC call number for *Theodore Rex* is 973.91. The number is in the 900 range, indicating that it is classified under history and geography. The second number identifies that the book is in the subcategory for North America, the 970s. The additional numbers add specificity to the identification.

Do not be chagrined if it all seems like too much to remember. The reference librarians at your library can help you decipher the systems and help you find books for your topic. If you have the author's name and title, they can readily retrieve the titles from the library stacks. If you have the call number, your search will be even easier. It simplifies the process.

In addition to the call number, the card also provides useful information about the title. Each card in the catalog offers a complement of information about the title that can help you determine just how useful it is likely to be. As seen in Figure 2.2, the cards also include information on:

1. The year of publication, useful in determining how timely the information will be.
2. The editions that are available in the library, useful in ensuring that you get the version you need.
3. Types of illustrations you will find in the book, useful if you are in need of photographs, maps, or diagrams.
4. The number of pages, useful in determining how much reading is required.
5. Its current availability in the library, useful in determining whether a visit to the shelf will be fruitful or whether you will need to order the book.

Browsing for Information

Knowing the category and subcategory designations for your topic also allows you to peruse the library shelves and browse titles in your subject area. Browsing is often useful in the early stages of your search for information because it allows you to open the books and scan the tables of contents, indexes, introductions, and chapter headings of books on your topic. These, in turn, can offer you a good idea of how helpful the work will be. Browsing, however, can be time-consuming.

To use your browsing time effectively, acquaint yourself with the categories under which you will likely find titles about your topic. Learn where the categories are shelved in the library. Typically, you will find topic labels or the range of call numbers for the topics in that aisle posted at the ends of individual aisles. After identifying the call numbers for your topic and subtopic, you will be able to go directly to the shelves where titles on your topic are located.

Keep in mind, however, that the best materials on your topic might not always be in the section where you are browsing. If a publication covers a variety of topics, it may be classified under one that is different from what you looked up.

Fortunately, subjects in card catalogs are cross-referenced so that you can search by title of the work, author's name, and a variety of keywords, as well as by subject. Your search will produce a record of the books with a "call number," or identification code. Libraries typically organize their shelves sequentially according to the system they use and label the ends of the aisles with the range of numbers to be found on the shelves in each aisle.

A Browsing Strategy

1. Identify the main category in the DDC or LCC system (whichever one your library uses) under which you are likely to find your topic.
2. Identify the logical subcategory under which your topic would fall.
3. Make a notation of the category and subcategory identification codes.
4. Use the first digit in the identification code to find your aisle.
5. Use the second digit in the code to identify the range of shelves containing titles on the subcategory.

6. Find titles that fit your topic.

7. Review the chapter headings, introduction, index, relevant pages, illustrations, and captions in the volume to identify how helpful the title will be.

8. As you browse through the shelves, remember that when the initial digits of the identification codes change, you'll be leaving your topic and moving into another.

Looking up Articles in Periodicals

Finding articles in periodicals that are relevant to your topic can be a bit trickier because they tend to be indexed in separate databases organized by subject.

Electronic look-ups provide the fastest and easiest way of finding articles, allowing you to search on the subject and keywords to zero in on your topic. Frequently, you begin at the same search form that you would use to find book titles. However, articles are usually found through databases that require a bit more searching because you may have to access more than one database to find what you are looking for.

To find articles and essays on your subject:

1. Review the list of databases and periodical indexes that are available at your library.

2. Identify the databases that might address your topic, such as Business Source Premier, for business articles, or MEDLINE for biomedical literature.

3. If you have difficulty finding an appropriate specialized database, use one such as Academic Search Premier or JSTOR which cuts across numerous categories.

4. Go to the search screen for your database.

5. Enter keywords to begin your search.
6. Select logical titles from the results that you receive.
7. Click on each title to retrieve the article citation.
8. Read the abstract, or summary, to see whether that article contains the type of information you are seeking.
9. Click to retrieve the full text if it is available electronically or use the citation information to order the article via e-mail or through your library.

Figure 2.3 shows an example of an article citation that was found in the Academic Search Premiere database.

Title:	**The Making of a Juggernaut.**
Source:	Fortune; 3/19/2007, Vol. 155 Issue 5, p104-104, 1/2p, 6 color
Document Type:	Article
Subject Terms:	*AUTOMOBILE industry & trade *HYBRID electric cars TOYOTA Motor Corp. TOYOTA automobiles SUPRA automobile TOYOTA Corolla automobile CAMRY automobile
Company/Entity:	TOYOTA Motor Corp. **Ticker:** TM
NAICS/Industry Codes:	336211 Motor Vehicle Body Manufacturing 423110 Automobile and Other Motor Vehicle Merchant Wholesalers
Abstract:	This article looks at popular *Toyota* automobiles from the 1950s to the 2000s. In 1950, *Toyota* exported the Crown and Land Cruiser; Toyopet Crown was the company's bestseller. In the 1980s, *Toyota* introduced a line of sports *cars*, including the Supra Turbo; the Corolla was its bestseller. In the 2000s, *Toyota's* answer to rising oil prices is the Prius hybrid-*electric* vehicle; the Camry is its bestseller.
Full Text Word Count:	177
ISSN:	00158259
Accession Number:	24341157
Persistent link to this record (Permalink):	https://login.proxy.libraries.rutgers.edu/login?url=http://search.ebsco
Database:	Academic Search Premier
View Links:	
Publisher Logo:	FORTUNE

Figure 2.3 Periodical databases such as the Academic Search Premiere offer a quick and easy way to look up articles in journals, magazines, and newspapers.

Note that it gives the title of the article and the source, the date of publication, volume and issue numbers, and information on the length, as well as the subject terms under which the article is cross-referenced. The abstract, which offers a short description of the information in the article, will be most helpful in identifying whether or not the article suits your research needs.

Many times, the citation will include a summary or abstract, which will give you a good idea of the contents of the article. Abstracts can help you identify which articles provide the most helpful information about your subject. For instance, Figure 2.3 shows a citation of an article that turned up in a search for information on electric cars that included the search terms "electric cars" and "Toyota." The abstract notes:

> This article looks at popular Toyota automobiles from the 1950s to the 2000s. In 1950, Toyota exported the Crown and Land Cruiser; Toyopet Crown was the company's bestseller. In the 1980s, Toyota introduced a line of sports cars, including the Supra Turbo; the Corolla was its bestseller. In the 2000s, Toyota's answer to rising oil prices is the Prius hybrid-electric vehicle; the Camry is its bestseller.

From the abstract, the researcher can determine that the article does discuss Toyota's electric hybrid but that it also includes historical information on Toyota models introduced since the 1950s. A researcher looking for information on how the hybrid enhances the company's image might determine from the abstract that this is a good article to use, while a researcher who is more interested in a general discussion of hybrid technology might want to continue the search.

A note of caution for beginning researchers is important here. Never confuse the abstract with the text of the article. The abstract is to help you in your search for information; it is not to be used as research. Remember that the abstract is simply a summary of what you will find in the article. It is not the article itself and, therefore, should never be quoted.

After using abstracts to identify the specific articles you want to use in your research, you will need to find the full text of the article. Many journals make full text available online. Note that in Figure 2.3, researchers can click on the "HTML Full Text" button to access the article. At times, full text is available in pdf files (electronic images) that can be ordered and delivered to you electronically via e-mail. When those options are not available, check with your librarian to see if the journal can be delivered from the library stacks or ordered through an interlibrary loan.

One useful way of identifying additional sources of information is to check the sources of quotations and citations in articles that were helpful to you. You then have the author's name, the title of the article, or the publication in which an article of interest might have appeared and can look it up using the same database you used to find the original article.

For instance, a quotation within an article you are referencing for a research paper on global warming might reference another article, stating: "According to a July 9, 2009, article in *The New York Times,* periodic warmings in the central Pacific Ocean contribute to hurricane activity in the Atlantic." You can then look up *The New York Times* article to see if it suggests if the conditions affecting the hurricanes are also linked to global warming.

To look up articles when you already know the title, name of the author, publication, or other information about it:

1. Review the list of databases and periodical indexes available at your library.

2. Identify databases that address the type of publication in which you might find the article you are seeking. If you were looking for *The New York Times,* for example, you would look for a general database that searched newspapers.

3. Go to the search screen for your database.

4. Enter as much information as you have about the article—the name of the author or publication or the title of the article, if you know them, or keywords from the phrases that captured your interest in the earlier article.

5. Browse the closest matches in the results that the search engine returns.

6. Click on the logical titles to retrieve the article citations and read the abstracts to identify your article.

7. Click to retrieve the full text if it is available electronically or use the citation information to have the article delivered to you via e-mail or through your library.

Identifying Appropriate Sources

Whether you found an article online or in print, you will need to evaluate the authority, or importance, of the research material you uncover.

Doing Your Research

As a general rule, reference texts, such as encyclopedias, dictionaries, and other standard reference sources like *Who's Who* or *Bartlett's Familiar Quotations* may meet the standard for high school papers but they are generally not acceptable in college research papers. The information in those volumes is considered "generic"—good for gathering general background but not unique or authoritative. Specialized dictionaries and compendiums, such as the *Physicians' Desk Reference*, a listing of FDA-approved drugs, represent the exception.

University professors prefer "primary" and "secondary" sources. Primary sources are ones with unique discussions of ideas, concepts, trends, events, personalities, and discoveries. They report findings, set forth arguments, and provide unique insights and conclusions from the authors who wrote them. Secondary sources are materials that use or report on the work of others to provide summaries, analyses, or interpretations of primary sources.

An example of a secondary source would be a book review or an analysis of another work. For example, *The Rights of Man*, Thomas Paine's famous essay in defense of the French Revolution, is a primary work. It sets forth his original argument against the French monarchy. An article that mentions the essay in a discussion about the ideas of philosophers in the 1700s would be considered a secondary source.

This is not to say that you should abandon encyclopedias and other standard references. Such sources make great starting points in your research. Not only do they provide valuable background on the topic you plan to discuss, but they reveal the wealth of information that is commonly known about the subject.

Encyclopedias can also point you to other valuable sources. Encyclopedia articles often contain their own bibliographies that cite the primary and secondary research sources that the encyclopedia writers and editors used to develop the article. Not only will these citations direct you to primary sources that can be useful in your own research, but they come from sources that you know were deemed reliable by the editors of the encyclopedia.

Identifying Reputable Online Sources

No matter how you access articles on the Internet, you should critically evaluate every publication you identify as a possible source in your research to determine its acceptability. Web sites for companies and special interest groups may provide a vast amount of information on your topic but, if the purpose of the Web site is to sell products related to the topic or advocate a particular position or point of view, it may not be useful for your purposes.

A discussion about the prognosis for those suffering from pancreatic cancer that appears on the Web site of the American Cancer Society, for instance, would be considered reliable for someone writing a research paper for a nursing class. However, if the discussion appeared on a commercial Web site of a company selling a purported miracle cure, it would not. It is important to identify who is publishing the article and why.

When you find an article, however, it is often difficult to determine just how well-informed the author was and how reliable the information is. Too often, the writers of the information and articles you find on a site are not even identified. So how do you determine how authoritative an article is?

Doing Your Research

Frequently, we can make that determination based on what we learned from our research. Ask yourself: Is this information consistent with what I have found elsewhere? Does it logically follow what I have already learned? If it does not and you still would like to use the information in your paper, expand your research to see if you can find other sources that support or confirm what it says.

Find out a bit about the author. Look for a biography next to, or at the bottom of, the article. Sometimes, the author's byline is hot-linked to a biography on another Web page. Avoid using blog posts and other sources by unnamed authors or authors using anonymous or fictitious "handles."

To identify publishers or sponsoring organizations, it is useful to visit the home page of the Web site that published the article. Often, you will find a "home page" button somewhere near the article that can take you there. If the home page offers little or no information about the publisher, look for an "About" link at the top, bottom, or side column of the home page. The "About" page should provide a mission statement and/or a history of the sponsoring group. You can often find this information on an FAQ (frequently asked questions) page.

It is also useful to know what type of Web site domain the article is from. The type of domain is indicated by the three-letter extension that follows the "dot" at the beginning of the Web address where the article is located. Common domain types include commercial (com), educational (edu), governmental (gov), and organizational (org). The official Web site of the U.S. president, for instance, is www.whitehouse.gov where the .gov stands for government. The official site of the American Cancer Society is www.cancer.org where the .org stands for organization.

Be especially wary of sites with extensions that are not consistent with the nature of the site. While gov means that you have arrived on a government-sponsored site, for instance, com usually means that you have arrived at a privately sponsored commercial site. For instance, www.whitehouse.com featured pornography until it was relaunched in 2004 as a video news site for reader contributors.

Know Your Web Sites

- com stands for commercial, and biz stands for business. These are business-sponsored sites. Their articles are usually designed to promote their products and brands and possibly sell you something.
- edu stands for education. These are school and university sites and often contain essays and articles written by teachers and professors.
- gov stands for government. These sites often present government-sponsored research, governmental records, and other official information about local, state, and federal governmental agencies.
- org stands for organizations; these can represent anything from research and support organizations, such as the American Cancer Society, to lobby groups with specific legislative agendas.
- int stands for international organization.
- eu, it, uk, ru, fr, and other two-letter codes are examples of country codes. The ones listed here stand for European Union, Italy, United Kingdom, Russia, and France, respectively. These do not always indicate that the site is

operated by a resident, business, or organization within that country, however; many countries allow persons and groups from outside the country to license the site names for outside commercial use.

Other clues at the Web site will be helpful. To get a sense of how well-researched or fact-checked an article may be, check for citations and hyperlinks that refer to sources with additional reading. These can include previously published articles, graphics, maps, and hyperlinks to outside references.

Publication dates are also important. Not only do they indicate how timely the information in the article is, but they provide a historical context when you need one. A report quoting eye-witnesses to the bombing of Pearl Harbor, the event that sparked the U.S. entry into World War II, may provide more specific details about the events as they unfolded than an analysis of events that was published 40 years later. Online newspapers and magazines usually include a "dateline" that identifies the date of publication at the top of the story, just under the headline. "Last updated" and copyright notices that appear at the bottom of Web pages can also help you identify when an article was published. If you have chosen a topic that demands up-to-date information, such as the United States' evolving policy toward stem cell research, it is often best to avoid articles where you cannot determine a date of publication. You cannot produce a credible paper if your research is out of date.

How to Identify Good Online Sources

- Does it come from a source my audience will recognize as an authority on the subject?

- Does it meet the requirements of the assignment?
- Will it meet my instructor's expectations?
- Am I getting facts or opinion?
- Does the information have a commercial purpose? Is it advertising, a press release, or promotional copy?
- Do the author's arguments seem logical, or do they overgeneralize or oversimplify?
- How well researched was the article?
- Are the sources of the article's information evident? What are they?
- What is the author's name? Avoid using sources by unnamed authors or authors using anonymous or fictitious "handles."
- What is the person's background? Does the author possess the experience, education, or authority to comment intelligently on the subject?
- Who is the publisher or the sponsoring organization?
- If it is an organization, what is its mission?
- When was the article written?
- Based on what you already know, does the article appear to make exaggerated claims?

Identifying Reputable Print Sources

Finding information in print sources can be equally as challenging as finding them online. Often the information you seek will be found in a small section of one article that appears in a very large volume. How do you find the information and know it will be useful unless you read the whole thing?

How to Find Good Print Resources

- Look up your topic in the book's index. Read those passages.
- Check journals and reports for an abstract, summary of findings, or executive summary at the beginning; these highlight the key information in the report.
- Review prefaces, introductions, and summaries on dust jackets for a quick overview.
- Read reviews, summaries, and commentaries about books.
- Check citations in a work to see how well-documented the work is.
- Read headlines, subheads, and call-outs in newspapers and magazines.
- Scan graphics and illustrations. Read the captions that accompany them.

Reading Critically

You cannot write intelligently about a subject if you have not fully read and understood the material you found in your research. This requires "critical" reading. Critical reading means more than reviewing and recording the material. It means pausing to think about it. Ask yourself whether you found the research convincing. Then ask yourself: Why or why not?

There are strategies for critical reading, just as there are for writing research papers. Critical reading requires you to gain a complete and accurate understanding of the material you find in your research so that you can analyze it intelligently and interpret it for others. This means devoting more time to the reading than you normally do when you sit down to casually read a newspaper or curl up with a novel.

Expect to spend more time with a text than what it takes to simply understand what it says. Think about what you read; ask yourself questions about it. Evaluate its logic. Consider alternatives to the information the author presented. Be prepared to turn to other texts if you do not find answers to your questions or if the author's arguments appear invalid. The more you can inform yourself about your topic and what other writers have said about it, the more you will equip yourself for the task ahead.

Critical reading is challenging so you will want to diminish noise and interferences. Turn off your radio, TV, iPod, and cell phone—anything that is likely to interrupt. Do not check your e-mail or read while socializing with friends. Reading in a quiet environment, and pursuing strategies for understanding eases the process and reduces the amount of time you will spend on research.

How to Create a Reading Environment

- Read at an appropriate time when you can devote the time and attention the material requires.
- Look for a quiet place where friends, family, or coworkers are not likely to interrupt you.
- Minimize distractions. Turn off your TV, radio, and cell phone. Let voicemail take your calls. Do not check text messages.
- Close the door to your room or office.

Before you can make up your own mind about a topic, you need to be aware of the arguments others have made both for and against it. Thousands of years ago, the Greek philosopher Aristotle identified three ways in which information is presented to persuade others to believe in what was written or said. They are: *ethos* (meaning ethical), *pathos* (meaning emotional), and *logos* (meaning logical).

- An *ethical argument* cites an authority whose experience or qualifications makes a statement believable.

  Example: Astronomer Dr. Josef Allen Hynek, a consultant to several studies of UFOs conducted by the U.S. Air Force, claimed there was "sufficient evidence" to believe in extraterrestrial intelligence.

- An *emotional argument* is designed to arouse the audience's emotions and experiences so that they identify with, and accept, the writer's proposition.

  Example: Imagine a child who will not live to see its twenty-first birthday and the parent who will not see that child graduate, get married, or have children. It is time to find a cure for this crippling illness.

- A *logical argument* makes a claim based on reasoning to persuade an audience to accept a writer's point of view.

  Example: Oxygen and hydrogen combine to form water. Therefore, water cannot exist on a planet that lacks oxygen in its atmosphere.

Appeals like the simple one shown below can be presented in a logical way but be completely invalid. It is up to you to determine their validity. Often that requires additional research.

Example: Time is money. Copper pennies are money. Therefore, time is forged from copper.

Use the form to identify an author's arguments and the data and claims used to make them. Outline the arguments that you think are the most persuasive. When you have finished outlining the arguments, ask yourself what you think about the topic. Do the author's appeals make sense? How would you evaluate them?

Evaluating Arguments

Book title_____

Author's name_____

Author's title, position, or experience_____

Emotional arguments (appeal to the audience's feelings)

1._____

_____

_____

2._____

_____

_____

_____

3._____

_____

_____

Ethical arguments (the author's expertise)

1._____

_____

_____

2._____

_____

_____

3._____

_____

_____

Logical arguments (information and ideas that support the author's conclusion)

1. _____

_____

_____

2. _____

_____

_____

3. _____

_____

_____

What I found most persuasive_____

_____

Documenting Your Research

Perfect research papers require that you accurately represent and cite the information you found in your research. Writers cite sources so that others can identify them and evaluate the relevance of the information. Just as you relied on other authors' citations to evaluate materials for your research, others will look for citations in your paper to evaluate yours.

Documenting sources is easiest when you do it as you identify the research sources you will use. Avoid making your bibliography or works cited the last thing you do in the writing process; it is too easy to forget the source of a significant fact or quotation. Retracing your sources to look things up all over again is difficult and time-consuming. Capture the information you will need for a bibliography or works cited as you look up the information.

Recording the information as you find it—in a log, on note cards, or in a word processing file on your computer, makes sense. It is useful to print Web articles you intend to use and to photocopy print pages you may reference. That way, you capture the author's exact words and see them in their exact context if you refer to them as you write.

It is useful to develop a strategy for keeping track of quotations, data, and other information you may cite as you write your paper. Use note cards—one per book or article—to record bibliographic information from that work. On each card, write down the name of the author (or authors); editor (if there is one); book title or article headline; name of the publication; publisher, place and year of publication; volume, issue, and page numbers (in the case of periodicals); along with the key ideas and quotations you expect to use from the publication. Use the rest of the card to record the information you expect to use in your paper. Be sure to use quotation marks around any exact wording and key ideas you might use in your paper and note the page numbers where you found them. That way, you will have kept an accurate record of your quotations, summaries, and their sources and will be able to copy them correctly into your paper, instead of having to re-research the material later to check your facts and ensure that you are avoiding plagiarism.

If you keep this information in a notebook, use a separate page for each resource; if you are recording it in a running log in a word processing document, allow plenty of room beneath each entry. That way you will have plenty of room to add relevant facts and quotations under the source. Do not hesitate to add pages or lines, as needed, to include additional information. Again, be sure to mark the quotations with quotation marks and record the page numbers on which you found the quotations and key ideas you record.

What to Document

- The author's (or authors') name (or names)
- The titles of the chapters, essays, or articles that you consulted within books and journals
- The name of the publisher
- The place of publication
- The year of publication
- Volume and issue numbers (if applicable)
- The page numbers where the information appeared
- Key ideas and information
- Key arguments

Keeping careful records of your research saves time and energy. It is much easier to gather details for your documentation as you access the data online or sit with the book open on your desk. If you wait until you have finished writing your paper and then go back to confirm the information, you will only be creating more work for yourself. Moreover, if you used articles that you found on the Internet, you risk the possibility that the Web pages were changed or removed after you found them.

How to Record Your Research

- Make copies of articles.
- Write the bibliographic information on the back.
- Use a marker to highlight key points, pertinent quotations, and interesting statements in your copies of the articles, as well as important names, places, and dates.
- Take notes as you read.

■ Summarize the highlighted information in your own words.

■ Write down your observations and questions about the material.

For online sources, it is a good idea to print the Web page and keep it as a paper record to refer to later. You can record source information as you collect it by opening a separate window with a blank word processing file where you can type in the information you will need (if you do this, be sure to give the file a relevant name that allows you to easily find it afterward).

What to Document for an Online Source

1. Headline or title of the article
2. The author's or editor's first and last name (or names if there is more than one)
3. Name of the online publication or Web site
4. Database or project you consulted (if applicable)
5. The publisher
6. The date on which the article was published or last revised
7. The date on which you accessed the source
8. The URL or Web address

The precise details and order in which these details will appear in the citation you use will vary according to the citation style the assignment requires you to follow. Most high school and freshman composition classes, as well as courses in colleges of arts and sciences require that students follow the Modern Language Association (MLA) style; other courses of study, particularly the sciences and many business programs, require American Psychological Association (APA) style. You will often find other styles, including the *Chicago Manual of Style* (CMS), which is typically followed by textbook and magazine publishers. A multitude of style guides, available in print and online, provide guidance on how to document your sources.

Later in this book, we talk more about them and point you to Web sites that will automatically generate properly formatted citations for you.

These helpful computerized tools are only as good as the information you enter into them. So it is important that you carefully and correctly record the information. Perfecting your note-taking skills as you conduct your research will help ensure the outcome.

Narrowing (or Expanding) Your Search

You cannot say everything there is to say about a general subject in a single research paper. Time and the page limits of your assignment, simply do not allow it, and papers that attempt to cover large topics with a broad brush, without saying anything in particular, typically earn low grades. Your instructor is looking for useful, specific information presented in well-focused arguments. Therefore, you have to narrow your topic and focus it on the particular aspect of it that you want to write about.

As you read, identify the ideas that you find interesting and unique and record those on your index card or in your word processor file. Not everything you discover in your research will be pertinent to your essay. Look for information that supports your position. For instance, a general topic such as "sex education," provides various avenues of research and discussion—from its role in promoting awareness of human sexuality to the political controversies that attend that mission. Either one of those is much too broad to cover in a single paper. Your challenge is to focus your topic in a way that tells your reader something interesting about it.

One way to do this is to pose a proposition for debate or a specific question that requires an answer. These can address particular political, theoretical, social, or economic aspects of the topic. For instance, using the sex education example, a student might ask: "How realistic are sex education programs that advocate abstinence?"

How to Narrow Your Topic

- Ask yourself a question that requires a specific answer.
- Pose a proposition that is open to debate.
- Focus on an interesting angle that you found in an analysis of your topic.

At other times, your research may come up wanting and you will have to expand your search. If you began with a very specific topic or one about which little has been written—such as the legitimacy of the eighth-century attempt by Charlemagne's oldest son, Pippin, to gain control of the Holy Roman Empire, for instance—you will need to expand your search. It is often easiest to do this by taking cues from the information found in your search. A student researching Pippin might address the attempted coup in terms of father-son relationships and relate psychological research to the issue.

How to Expand Your Topic

- Complete a keyword search, using words or phrases that describe your topic.
- Choose two or three of the search results and read those articles.
- Look for relevant hyperlinks within the articles and visit those.
- Note unique terms and phrases used within the article; these will often suggest terms that you can use to make additional searches.

Writing Annotated Bibliographies

Many times an assignment will ask you to produce an "annotated bibliography" of your research sources. Even if your assignment does not require this, it is a good idea to produce one so that you have a record of your research and the sources it came from. In any event, you will need it later as you assemble the bibliography or works cited in your final draft.

An annotated bibliography is a list of the references you consulted in your research, including the author's name, title of the article, title of the book or publication, publisher, etc. However, an annotated bibliography also includes a short summary, synopsis, or abstract of the book or article. If your assignment does not require you to produce an annotated bibliography as part of your research paper, it is still helpful to do one. Annotated bibliographies help you document your sources and provide excellent references when you sit down to write. They also help you develop deeper insights into your topic because you will see what has already been written about it.

How to Write an Annotated Bibliography

- Identify the topic.
- Highlight the author's thesis or main point.
- Highlight the author's central arguments in support of the thesis.
- Present your response to the author and the source. Did they seem reliable? Why or why not?
- Present your response to the article. Did it answer your questions? What questions do you still have? Did it complement your other research? Did it expand your knowledge of your topic?
- Write in clear, distinct sentences so that neither you nor your reader will have trouble interpreting your remarks.

Most annotated bibliographies are written as a citation in the style specified by your assignment (MLA, APA, or CMS) with a paragraph (or several paragraphs) of summary and analysis following the citation. For instance, an annotated bibliographic reference to Charles Darwin's *Origin of the Species,* written in MLA style, might look like this:

Darwin, Charles. "Introduction." <u>Origin of the Species.</u> Literature.org: The Online Library. 18 Apr. 2009 <http://www.literature.org/authors/darwin-charles/the-origin-of-species/introduction.html>.
Summary: This controversial book, published in 1859, is the one in which Darwin presented his theory of natural

selection. Based on observations he made as a naturalist on an around-the-world voyage aboard H.M.S. Beagle, the book is a compendium of biological observations and conclusions based upon them. Darwin speaks of his conviction "that species are not immutable." He adds that "Natural Selection has been the main but not exclusive means of [genetic] modification."

Conducting Original Research

Original research is research you conduct rather than find in books or articles. It is also called primary research because it starts with you. If you plan to conduct primary research, like an experiment, personal interviews, or a survey of people, you will need to devise a basic methodology for your inquiry.

A methodology is simply a statement of the procedure you will follow in conducting the research. Depending upon the type of research you are conducting, the methodology could include:

- A step-by-step sequence of procedures performed for an experiment.
- Questions to be asked in personal interviews.
- The names of people you plan to interview or a profile of the people you plan to interview.
- The questionnaire you will use in the interview.
- A demographic profile that segments people you will survey by such things as age range, gender, educational levels, income bracket, geographic location, or common interests

A good methodolocy lends credibility to your project. If you are conducting an experiment, for instance, it is important to record the process so that others can later repeat the experiment and get the same results. It also provides important background for your readers and ensures consistency across your results. Whenever you conduct interviews, your readers will be interested in what questions you asked and what the person answered. If you are conducting a survey, it is important to ask everyone in the survey the same questions so that you can compare responses. It is also essential to note whom you surveyed so that you can say something about the attitudes of the particular group. For instance: *Eighty-four out of one hundred students polled at Jupiter University said that smoking should be banned completely from campus.*

Interviews and surveys can add weight and credibility to your research paper. Analytical papers benefit from the comments of an expert's informed opinion. The social sciences, in particular, make frequent use of interviews and surveys to assess trends in attitudes and public opinion. You can achieve this using "secondary research"—interviews that appear in newspapers and magazines and reports on the existing surveys and opinion polls such as those conducted by the Gallup and Harris polling organizations.

It is often useful, however, to conduct "primary research" or original research such as surveys, interviews, and fieldwork that you design and conduct. Very often, the research you conduct will be the topic of your paper, and your own results will provide the substance of evidence for your hypothesis. This is particularly true in the sciences and in many fields of business, including marketing, management, and labor relations.

Surveys and interviews are also useful when you want to expand upon the findings you found in secondary research. For instance, suppose you cited a national poll regarding people's attitudes toward a current political issue. You could develop a survey to gather local opinion or to further assess attitudes of a particular demographic. It might also be useful to conduct a sampling of interviews to gain quotations and other anecdotal information within your local community.

Surveys

Fortunately, Web sites and software programs abound to help you design surveys by offering a structure for organizing the survey, prompting you to enter questions, and tabulating the results. Online free polling services include zoomerang.com, and polldaddy.com. *The New York Times* offers a lesson on poll creation, called "To Free or Not Too Free," for middle school and high school teachers in its Learning Network at www.nytimes.com/learning/index.html.

Surveys should be carefully focused and ask specific questions to minimize ambiguities or bias in the findings. Questions should be crafted and presented to ensure that the data you collect will allow you to make the kinds of determinations you seek. Surveys should follow a structure that informs respondents of the purpose.

Structuring Your Survey

1. Give your survey a title.
2. State the purpose of the survey.
3. Tell respondents where the information will be published.

4. Include a privacy statement explaining with whom you will share the information and how it will be used.
5. Get the respondents' permission to use the data they provide.
6. Describe how the survey will be conducted.
7. Set a deadline for when you need the results.
8. Tell the respondents how to complete the survey. Be very clear about how they should answer the questions (i.e., whether they should check, circle, or underline the answer or write a response in the blank provided).
9. Thank respondents for their time.

You want the respondents to complete the surveys. For that reason, the surveys should not be too long. Aim for 25 to 30 questions. The choices presented to respondents should be straightforward and easy to respond to. Questions can be presented in the following ways.

1. Yes or no/true or false
2. Multiple choice
3. Ratings on a scale, usually 1 to 10
4. Ranking in order of importance or preference
5. Comments

Yes-no and true-false questions are the most straightforward. Multiple choice questions can be problematic if the respondent does not identify with the choices given; these should always include options such as "don't know" or "none of the above" that leave room for exceptions. Rankings allow respondents to express qualitative preferences by assigning a number that reflects their attitudes according to a scale.

Rankings, on the other hand, ask the respondent to place a series of items in order. Comments can be the most revealing as they ask the respondent to state their opinions or describe something; however, they are difficult to tabulate as the results cannot be easily fitted into categories.

As you begin designing questions, ask yourself: What, exactly, do I want to determine? Surveys are typically conducted for one of two different reasons.

Attitude surveys can be short and simple, focused around a single issue and pose a single question or a short set of questions. For instance:

Do you believe that the quality of education would improve if the school year was lengthened to offer more hours for instruction?

Yes

No

Surveys designed to identify trends tend to be much longer than other kinds of surveys. This is to provide a qualitative view of related issues rather than one that is simply based on a yes or no answer. For instance:

1. How would you rate the quality of education in your local school district?
   a. Excellent
   b. Good
   c. Average
   d. Below average
   e. Poor

2. Which of the factors listed below do you believe has the greatest impact on the quality of education in your district? (Select one)
   a. Number of hours students spend in class
   b. Class size
   c. Teacher training
   d. Administrative control
   e. Parental/community support

   If you answered a to this question (number of hours students spend in class), please answer the following questions. If you answered b, c, or d, please skip to question 6.

3. Do you think your local school district should add class hours to the daily schedule?
   a. Yes
   b. No

4. How many hours do children in your school district spend in school?
   a. Fewer than five
   b. Five
   c. Six
   d. More than six
   e. Don't know

5. How much time do you think should be added to the school day in your district?
   a. 30 minutes
   b. 1 hour
   c. 90 minutes
   d. 2 hours
   e. More than 2 hours

Adding questions that gather demographic data allows you to make distinctions about the individuals being polled and interpret their answers according to group affiliations. For instance, the survey in this example might also ask whether the respondent is a parent, male or female, whether the person currently has children in school and, if so, the ages of the children. Answers to questions can then be cross-referenced with the demographic data to make interpretations such as:

"Eighty-one percent of mothers with children currently attending school five hours per day said that they believe their children are receiving a good to excellent education."

Questions asking the person's age range or income can also be relevant, but such questions should always be respectful of peoples' privacy. Rather than ask survey respondents to divulge their sex or annual income, for instance, present the respondents with a range and give them the option of not answering, such as:

Are you:
a. male
b. female
c. I prefer not to answer
What is your annual income?
a. under $25,000
b. $25,001–$50,000
c. $50,001–$75,000
d. $75,001–$100,000
e. Over $100,000
f. I prefer not to answer

Tabulating Survey Results

A great deal of care should be taken to correctly tabulate results. This can be a challenging task if you have not collected data through an online site or from a form that provides automatic analysis. Researchers who expect to review and tabulate the data themselves would be well advised to work with a small group of respondents (no more than 20) to keep the task manageable.

The American Statistical Association (ASA) and the American Psychological Association (APA) publish excellent guidelines on how to conduct surveys and tabulate the results. The ASA's publication *What Is a Survey?* can be downloaded from www.whatisasurvey.info. The APA offers numerous articles on conducting surveys at its Web site, www.apa.org.

Interviews

Getting an interview is usually not as difficult as it may, at first, seem. Groups and individuals welcome the opportunity to express themselves and talk about their causes, products, and services in public forums.

Often, you can find subjects to interview via the Web sites you visit in your research. Use the *contact* form at the Web site to extend your invitation. Allow plenty of time. If you want to interview the person who runs the site, he or she may get back to you immediately. However, most often your request will have to be forwarded to an appropriate individual or routed through "channels," usually the public relations office of the sponsoring organization.

Arranging Interviews

1. Identify whom you will interview.

2. Locate and contact the person.

3. Invite his or her participation.

4. Determine how you will interview the person—by phone, in person, or by e-mail.

5. Assemble the questions you will ask.

6. Forward the questions to your interviewee.

7. Request the right to ask follow-up questions.

Identifying and Contacting Experts

Profnet is a service run by the Public Relations Society of America (PRSA). Originally designed to connect newspaper and magazine reporters to experts within its member companies, it is now open to academic and corporate researchers, analysts, bloggers, publishers, authors, and consultants. There you can browse a database of more than 25,000 expert profiles to identify someone you would like to interview or send a query asking experts in that area to respond. After receiving responses, you will need to determine whom to interview. Pick people whose backgrounds and areas of expertise are most relevant to your topic. You will find the Profnet Web site at: www.profnet.prnewswire.com.

WritersWeekly.com, the online site for *Writers Weekly* magazine, a publication for freelance journalists, also allows you to post requests for interviews in its forum. Requests are also published in the site's weekly newsletter. This is a good resource when you are looking for candid, person-on-the-street types of responses. You will find the forum at www.forums.writersweekly.com.

If you are a student, you may find that the best expert on your topic is just around the corner. Experts in all fields can be found on the faculties of colleges and universities, particularly major research universities. Take your request to the public relations office at your university. PR officers can help you identify and set up appointments with faculty experts who are available for interviews.

Other good sources are book publishers and literary agents, particularly if an expert has recently published a book and is trying to draw attention to it. For instance, McGraw-Hill publishes a list of its author-experts at the following Web site, along with a form you can fill out to request an interview: www.authorexperts.ca.

You can find other author-experts by simply doing an online search of the words "author" and "expert." When you've found an author who is an expert on your topic, you can use the site's "contact" information to request an interview. Be specific when requesting an interview. Compose a short, friendly, well-written e-mail and include all the information that the publisher and potential interviewee will need in order to understand your topic and the issues you plan to address.

Guidelines for Requesting Interviews

1. Identify yourself by full name and title. For instance: "My name is Jane Doe. I am a graduate student in Criminal Justice at Rutgers University."
2. Explain your assignment/project. For instance: "I am conducting research for my masters' thesis."
3. Explain your topic. For instance: "I am researching trends in social networking."

4. State your time frame. For instance: "I plan to complete my interviews for this project by October 31."

5. Offer an idea of how much time the person should allow for the interview. For instance: "The interview should take approximately 20 minutes."

6. Ask for the interview, requesting either someone who is able to speak to your topic or a specific interviewee by name. For instance: "I would like to interview Julian Sharp, author of *Design and Launch an Online Social Networking Business in a Week*."

7. Provide your contact information. For instance: "You may contact me at (phone number) or at my e-mail address (e-mail address)."

8. Finish with a cordial closing as you would in a letter. For instance: "Sincerely yours, Jane Doe."

9. A day or two before the interview, send an e-mail reminder or telephone the interviewee to confirm the time and date.

Interviews can be conducted via e-mail, by telephone, or in person. There are advantages and disadvantages to each method. E-mail interviews are convenient; interviewees can respond at their convenience. They also provide you and the interviewee with a written record of what was asked and answered. However, they also place a burden on the inter viewee by requiring the person to write out responses that you normally would record in a telephone or face-to-face interview. Be prepared to give considerable thought to questions you prepare in advance. Follow-up questions are difficult in e-mail and you do not want to waste the time of people who have graciously agreed to be interviewed. Be specific and complete in your questions to avoid getting answers that require follow-up because they do not deliver the information you need. Avoid questions like, "What do you think of social networking?" Instead, be specific with questions that seek detailed information, such as, "What is the most significant trend in social networking that you see emerging among teenagers, and why do you believe it's the most significant?"

Telephone interviews are more open-ended and offer you the opportunity to follow up with questions that might occur to you in the course of the conversation. They are not good options, however, if you are excessively shy or if the interviewee is uncomfortable with them. They can also be difficult to arrange if the person maintains a busy schedule. Never insist on a telephone interview; choose the format that is most convenient for the interviewee. Finally, it is useful to record telephone interviews so that you can later review what was said and ensure accuracy on any quotes you use; however, always ask the permission of the interviewee before recording an interview.

Face-to-face interviews, like telephone interviews, are not for the shy and can be difficult to arrange. However, they offer you the opportunity to meet the interviewee. This can be particularly valuable if you are meeting in a setting that is pertinent to your course of inquiry, such as the person's laboratory or a social setting that pertains to the topic, such as an Internet café if you are discussing social networking, or a troubled housing project if you are discussing the influence of neighborhood environments on high school completion rates, crime rates, or family support networks. Ask the person's permission to record the interview at the time you make the appointment.

Doing Your Research

If you are doing a telephone or face-to-face interview, be sure you allow the interviewee to do the talking. Do not interrupt or rush the person through the interview. Many times, interviewees will use the opportunity to promote recent books, writings, or product/service introductions. If they do, let them and then proceed to the questions that are of interest to you. Cutting off an interviewee can set a bad tone for the interview and produce disappointing results.

As you incorporate interviews in your paper, you must accurately and fairly present their views and opinions—even when they do not conform to your own. Be sure to do your research in advance. Read at least one thing your interviewee has written on the topic. Have a good sense in advance of what the person will say about it.

At times, interviewees will ask for a copy of your final paper. Often, this will be a condition that is discussed before the interview is granted. If you have agreed to provide a copy, do so. Always respect the requests of the interviewee.

Chapter 3

Crafting Your Outline

Before you begin to write a paper, you must identify the thesis or main point of what you plan to present and then select and organize the ideas and information you will include to support or "prove" it. Many times, writers will "prewrite" before they begin to write a research paper. Prewriting is what you do to prepare yourself for producing your paper. Prewriting begins with brainstorming, or thinking about what your research has taught you, and organizing it into an outline. It requires thoughtful review and attention to how you will organize your discoveries, ideas, and opinions within the paper.

If you have ever watched a professional golfer or tennis player prepare for a championship match, you have seen concentration in action. A hush comes over the audience and the pro is entirely focused on the task ahead. Believe it or not, writing is also like that. It requires concentration.

Writing requires a great deal of thought to allow your thoughts to flow. That means getting those thoughts down so that you can begin the real work of presenting them clearly and logically in your paper. Your first step in organizing the paper should be to brainstorm. Identify what you found interesting or surprising in your research, what you think about it, and why you think it.

Visual aids can be helpful. Bubble charts use connect-the-dot style patterns to illustrate relationships among your findings. Venn diagrams, such as those used to plot intersecting sets in algebra, can be used to help identify points of agreement and common ideas that you found in various research sources. Indented outlines offer a methodical procedure for structuring a paper by plotting out the topics to be discussed and the points to be made to support them.

All writers eventually develop their own techniques for brainstorming. Some of the most common methods to jump-start thinking include lists, bubble charts, and diagrams that identify and connect important points from the research to illustrate their relationships. It does not really matter how you brainstorm; pick a method that works well for you. The key is to find a way that helps you record your ideas that can be developed into an outline for the paper. This process is often called "prewriting."

Some instructors make prewriting part of the assignment and ask students to hand in the free-writing exercises and outlines they used to produce their papers.

How to Prewrite

- Find a quiet place where you are not likely to be interrupted.

- Put your iPod in the drawer. Turn off the TV, radio, and your cell phone. Resist the temptation to check e-mail, answer IMs, or visit your favorite Web site.

- Allot yourself a window of time—at least 15 minutes but, preferably, 30—to jot down everything you know and think about your topic.

- Record your thoughts in the way that is most comfortable for you.

- Do not edit yourself. Do not touch the spell-checker, and do not worry about correcting grammar or punctuation.

As you organize your research in preparation for writing your paper, you should give careful thought to exactly what you should include and to the best way to include it. Do not try to include everything you learned from your research. Much of it will not be relevant to your assignment. Also, all the most simplistic research papers (a book report, for instance, or a short summary of an experiment or an experience) will require you to structure the paper around key insights you gained or opinions you formed. It requires more than simply stringing together paragraphs that summarize your research.

Focus on the research that best supports your discussion, findings, or argument. You are more likely to get a higher grade by making good use of a limited number of research sources than by turning in a paper that is no more than a string of summaries of all the sources you consulted. Remember, research papers are exercises in quality—not quantity. Your ability to use your research to support and enhance the quality of your discussion is what counts. The prewriting exercises you do to structure the information should be directed at filtering out information that is irrelevant to your insights or point of view and focusing on building a strong case for what you choose to include.

Making Lists

Lists are great when you want to assemble information and ideas in order to compare and contrast them or to group or classify them in categories. They are also easy to produce once we have the information. Most of us are inveterate list makers, even in our everyday lives. So make a list and check it twice before writing—first to get your information down and, second, to begin to organize it logically so that a reader can follow your line of thinking.

How to Organize Your List

- List the most interesting things you learned in your research in order of their importance.
- Leave plenty of white space between the points on your list so that you can add information later.

- Review the list.

- Check to see that your list includes all the key points you learned in your research.

- Change the order of items on your list to ensure that the most important information is at the top and to group related ideas and information together.

Making Charts

Almost any fact you find in your research is likely to be interesting to someone, and you can usually find a way to use it. It must be relevant to your topic and the arguments you will use to persuade others that your views on the topic are noteworthy. Your facts must be arranged in a way your audience will find meaningful. They need to do more than simply summarize your findings. They should show your audience the implications of your findings and point out why they are relevant to readers' lives.

Bubble charts and Venn diagrams allow you to organize information visually so that you can easily identify common themes, information, and relationships in the information you have discovered.

Bubble charts, like the one in Figure 3.1, look like big connect-the-dots drawings. They are especially useful in helping to identify relationships. Lines and arrows connecting related clusters in a bubble chart show which ideas go together.

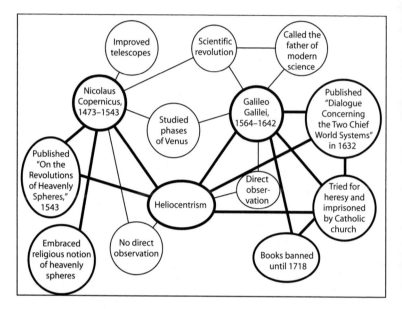

Figure 3.1 Bubble charts allow you to map relationships among ideas.

How to Create a Bubble Chart

- Write your topic in the middle of a piece of paper.
- Think of the most interesting things you learned about it.
- Write those things down, circling the topic to look like a "bubble."
- As you think of more and more things, keep writing them down, circling the topic.
- When you are finished, draw lines or arrows between bubbles with related information to point out common themes, ideas, arguments, and relationships.

Using a bubble chart to connect the facts and ideas you uncovered in your research helps you identify the relationships in the information you found, form conclusions about it, and construct persuasive arguments that will make your paper more meaningful to readers.

Venn diagrams, on the other hand, show overlapping themes and facts. They reveal commonalities and differences that can be used to make comparisons and contrasts, as shown in Figure 3.2

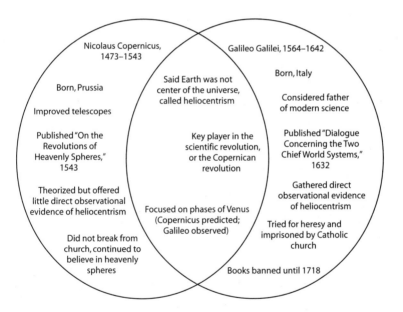

Figure 3.2 Venn diagrams allow you to see intersecting ideas and information.

Creating an Outline

After you have identified the ideas, relationships, and sets of facts you intend to use in your paper, it is time to organize them into an outline. An outline allows you to begin to structure your information in the order you will present it in your paper.

Outlining begins with a review of the lists, charts, or diagrams you created as prewriting exercises. It provides a way of determining which ones you will use in your paper.

Your outline, like your paper, will be organized around a thesis. The thesis is the main point of the paper or, if you are writing a persuasive paper, a claim you will make based on your research. The paragraphs that follow will be constructed to sustain the thesis with supporting evidence. This will be quotations, examples, descriptions, or anecdotes from your research.

How to Organize Your Outline

- Identify a thesis and list it as your main point. Later, it will provide the topic of your introduction, the first paragraph of your paper.

- In order of their importance, list the most interesting points from your research that support the thesis. These will be the topics of supporting paragraphs. Leave plenty of white space between points so you can list evidence that supports them.

- Use the white space under each point to list the evidence that supports that point. Use only the most relevant and interesting information.

- Edit your list.

- If one point seems to repeat another or there are close similarities, rewrite them as one point that groups related information.
- List your points in order of importance.
- Add a final point identifying the conclusion you want your readers to draw from the evidence or the most important observation they should make.
- Under it, list the reasons why.

Identifying a Thesis

The thesis is arguably the most important sentence in the paper, but, at this point, it is still a work in progress. You will change it to focus it and make it stronger when you write your draft. You will change it again as you revise and refine it in the editing process. The purpose of producing a working thesis for an outline is to get you started, to jumpstart your thinking.

This working thesis should be different from the subject, or topic, of your paper. It must do more than simply state "This paper is about …" A good thesis includes the most important information your reader should know. It may identify key themes or state a position, hypothesis, theory, opinion, or point of view that the paper is designed to defend, advocate, or argue. The type of paper you are writing will determine what the thesis should address:

- A thesis for a summary, such as a book report, should highlight the most important theme, opinion, or point of the reading.

- A thesis for a narrative, or story, should set the mood, state the theme, or identify the purpose in telling the tale.

- A thesis for a description or process paper should state the purpose and outcome of the process or experiment that is about to be described and highlight what was surprising or significant about it.

- A thesis for a persuasive paper should present the opinion or point of view that you want the reader to adopt.

It is always tempting to begin on a note that everyone can agree with, but this is not what you want to do when presenting research. A thesis should always be to the point. Make it as specific as possible and avoid making general statements or obvious observations. Your audience wants a thesis that will show them why they should read the paper. What will they learn? What makes it important? The thesis is usually presented in a single sentence that appears near the end of the introduction, the first paragraph of your paper. The body of the paper, the paragraphs that follow, will present the evidence that "proves" the thesis or, in the case of summaries and descriptions, completes a picture for the reader.

The thesis must also do more than simply restate or summarize the background you were given in the assignment. It should reveal the most important thing you learned from your research. You should avoid referencing yourself in the thesis (using personal pronouns such as I, me, or my). A good thesis is not just an opinion; it states what you concluded from the research you conducted.

For instance, in the examples below, the weak thesis simply tells readers the paper is about *The Adventures of Huckleberry Finn*; readers will expect to see a summary follow but not much else. The strong thesis not only signals that the paper will be about *The Adventures of Huckleberry Finn*, but it presents the opinion that the book's strong regional characteristics are what makes it a great American novel. Readers will expect the paper to present evidence to back up that claim.

> *Weak thesis:* This paper is about Mark Twain's *The Adventures of Huckleberry Finn*.

> *Strong thesis:* The use of local American dialects and strong regional characterizations in *The Adventures of Huckleberry Finn* have earned Mark Twain's book a place in the ranks of great American novels.

Tips for Writing Successful Thesis Statements

- The thesis should make a strong point about your topic; it should not simply name a topic.

- The thesis should express a proposition, opinion, or point of view. It should not simply repeat facts or summarize findings.

- The thesis should be specific. It should avoid vague or universal statements and avoid absolute or all-inclusive words such as "everyone," "everything," "good," or "successful."

- The thesis should show readers why they should care about the subject. It should catch their interest and encourage them to read to the end.

Identifying Topics and Arguments

The body of a research paper contains evidence that supports the thesis and shows why it is correct. In a persuasive paper, that evidence often takes the form of "arguments" aimed at convincing a reader to accept the opinion the writer expressed in the thesis. Arguments in a persuasive paper are not like quarrels you have with another person. There is no place for name-calling and personal attacks in a research paper. The arguments must be supported by what you uncovered in your research.

Just as you identified the arguments in other writers' work when you were doing your research, you must now identify the arguments you will use to support your thesis as you assemble your outline. Just as you looked for logical, emotional, and ethical arguments when you researched others' work, you must now create them to make your own research paper convincing:

- Your *logical arguments* should be presented in a rational order to make the thesis convincing. Logical arguments are usually based on facts, examples, and data that support the outcome that is predicted or advocated by the thesis.

- Your *emotional arguments* should appeal to readers' feelings. Emotional arguments are often based on examples or stories and anecdotes that move readers to support the thesis. They typically use vivid descriptions to help readers personally relate to the thesis.

- Your *ethical arguments* should establish the authority of your research by identifying and quoting or paraphrasing experts on the subject.

Crafting Your Outline

Write a short phrase in each of the blanks on the work sheet below to identify arguments you could use in your paper. List as many as come to mind. Depending upon your subject, you may have more of one type than another.

Arguments Worksheet

Logical arguments based on evidence from my research:

1. _____

_____

_____

_____

2. _____

_____

_____

_____

3. _____

_____

_____

_____

Emotional arguments that will appeal to my audience's feelings:

1. _____

_____

_____

_____

2. _____

_____

_____

_____

3. _____

_____

_____

_____

Ethical arguments that establish my expertise in the subject:

1. _____

_____

_____

_____

2. _____

_____

_____

_____

3. _____

_____

_____

_____

Outlining a Five-Paragraph Paper

High school writing teachers often use the "five-paragraph essay" as a standard format to help beginning writers structure their essays. It provides a solid, basic way of structuring short papers and makes it easy to organize the ideas you explored in your lists, charts, and worksheets.

A five-paragraph essay follows a simple structure. It begins with an introduction that contains the thesis, followed by three paragraphs that comprise the body of the essay. Each paragraph should address a separate topic supporting the thesis. The essay finishes with a concluding paragraph that reminds the reader of the thesis and, depending upon the nature of the essay, summarizes findings, concludes an analysis, or adds a call to action.

Paragraph 1: Introduction/thesis
Paragraph 2: First point, description, or argument
Paragraph 3: Second point, description, or argument
Paragraph 4: Third point, description, or argument
Paragraph 5: Conclusion

One of the keys to writing a successful five-paragraph essay is to ensure that there are smooth transitions from the introduction to the first argument or paragraph topic, as well as smooth transitions from one paragraph to the next, and to ensure that there is adequate evidence within each paragraph to support its topic, or the argument it makes.

The first sentence of your second paragraph should continue the transition from the end of your introduction to your first paragraph. The first sentence of the second paragraph is usually the "topic sentence" that presents the key fact, observation, point, or argument that will be discussed in the rest of the paragraph. The topic sentence is followed by evidence (quotations, summaries, examples, and data) that support or "prove" the topic. The final sentence of the paragraph should provide a transition to the next paragraph.

The third and fourth paragraphs follow the same format as the second:

- Topic sentence
- Evidence
- Transition

The fifth paragraph is the conclusion. It should remind the reader of the thesis and reemphasize its importance. In a narrative, it is the end of the story. In a descriptive or process paper, it presents a result. In a persuasive essay, it restates your opinion and often makes suggestions or recommendations about how you hope the reader will respond to the information presented.

The opening sentence in any conclusion should not merely pick up on the transition from the previous paragraph and hook back to the thesis; it should also do more than simply restate it. The conclusion should reflect on the thesis and the three points that you made in the preceding paragraphs. It should end with the idea that you want to leave with your reader.

How to Outline a Five-Paragraph Essay

Paragraph 1 (Introduction):

- Write a sentence that introduces your subject.
- Write a sentence that explains the importance of your subject.
- Write the thesis, a sentence that appears near the end of your introduction, stating the key point you want to make about the subject of your paper. This will be your thesis statement.

- Write a sentence that provides a smooth transition, or connection, to the first topic you will present in support of your thesis.

Paragraph 2 (Body)

- Write a topic sentence that introduces the most important observation from your research that supports your thesis.
- Present a quotation, example, or argument that supports the topic.
- Write a transition sentence that suggests, or is linked to, the next topic.

Paragraph 3 (Body)

- Write a topic sentence that introduces the second most important topic you will present in support of your thesis.
- Present a quotation, example, or argument that supports the topic.
- Write a transition sentence to the next topic.

Paragraph 4 (Body)

- Write a topic sentence that introduces the third topic you will present in support of your thesis.
- Present a quotation, example, or argument that supports the topic.
- Write a transition sentence to the conclusion.

Paragraph 5 (Conclusion)

- Summarize the evidence or arguments presented in the three preceding paragraphs.

- Write a sentence that reintroduces, or restates, your thesis using different words.
- Write a sentence that identifies what you want readers to learn from your paper or how you want them to act on your findings.

Expanding beyond Five Paragraphs

The five-paragraph format is commonly taught in high schools, but you will quickly outgrow it in college where extensive research cannot be represented in a mere five paragraphs and assigned page lengths stretch to ten pages or more. Papers grow to accommodate additional information or to meet the guidelines of the assignment. Five paragraphs, for instance, would be unacceptable in a ten-page paper. Each paragraph would cover approximately two pages and would be challenging to find enough evidence to make arguments without repeating yourself. The key is not to let the formula dictate what you write but to let the writing dictate the formula. You do not want to begin filling your research paper with useless information or long and wordy sentences just to fill up paragraphs. In a perfect research paper, you want to say what you want—and need—to say without repeating yourself or heading off on tangents that have little or nothing to do with your thesis.

It is far better to build your analysis by exploring, and discussing the implications of, additional topics than it is to belabor a few. You can add topics to support your thesis by using the following guide for each additional topic (paragraph) you add to your paper.

New Paragraph (Body)

- Write a topic sentence that introduces the next most important observation from your research that supports your thesis.

- Present a quotation, example, or argument as evidence to support that topic.

- Build on the topic with additional sentences that explore, analyze, or interpret the evidence you presented.

- Write a transition sentence that suggests, or is linked to, the next topic.

Continue to follow the same format for the body of the paper as you did above until you have fully explored your subject and presented the evidence and arguments you need to support your thesis.

Comparing and Contrasting Ideas and Information

Any good research paper should compare and contrast ideas and information on various sides of the issue or topic it explores. Comparisons expand readers' awareness of a subject and help them understand how it is similar or different from other ideas, events, or propositions. Instructors will often make an entire assignment a "compare and contrast" paper to determine how critically you examined your research, how well you understood it, and how well you can distinguish different ideas, data, and observations when presenting it to others.

Compare/contrast papers typically follow one of two different structures:

1. Using separate paragraphs to fully discuss one idea, then fully discuss another, and then make comparisons between the two. This is a straight-forward, easy-to-follow format that tends to work well for high school assignments that call for summaries or personal opinions. It is less useful for college papers that demand expanded discussions and greater analysis to support a thesis.

2. Integrating comparative and contrasting information into the discussions within the paragraphs. This format requires you to think about how to connect the ideas and information in the arguments you are presenting. It is effective when you need to present an integrated analysis or explore a variety of ideas.

Comparing and Contrasting in Separate Paragraphs

- Introduction.
- Body paragraph—topic 1: In a five-paragraph essay, you would explore your first topic in a single paragraph (the second paragraph in your paper). In a longer paper, you might use additional paragraphs to discuss distinct sub-topics. Do not introduce a new topic until you have fully explored the evidence that is required to make an effective presentation of this first one.
- Body paragraph—topic 2: In a five-paragraph essay, explore your second topic in the third paragraph of the paper. In a longer paper, discuss distinct aspects of the second topic using additional paragraphs until you have fully explored topic 2…

- Body paragraph—Begin making comparisons: After fully exploring each of the two topics in distinct discussions, as you did above, begin to compare them. In a five-paragraph essay, you would do this in your fourth paragraph. In a longer paper, you would tackle each point-by-point comparison in a separate paragraph.

Comparing and Contrasting within Paragraphs

- Introduction

- First point of comparison: Select the most important point your research sources discussed. Your topic sentence should tell what it is. Follow that by exploring various aspects of the discussions. Tell what key sources had to say about the topic. Point out the similarities and differences, identifying which ones possess the greatest merit and which possess the least. Finish with a transition sentence that takes the reader to the next point of comparison.

- Second point of comparison: Select the next most important point of comparison or contrast. Write a topic sentence that identifies it and why it is important. Again, contrast your various sources' slant on the topic and finish with a transition sentence leading to the next most important point.

- Third, fourth, fifth (and more) points of comparison: Continue as you did above, adding paragraphs as necessary until you have covered all the comparisons you want to make.

- Conclusion.

Comparisons and contrasts are important parts of almost any research paper, even when the paper is not assigned as a "compare/contrast" paper. Persuasive essays, in particular, should compare ideas and propositions to point out the disadvantages and advantages of one over the other. A process paper in which you are describing an experiment might include a comparison of two different reactions. Even a summary paper, such as a book report, might include a comparison of two different characters or themes in the story.

Chapter 4

Preparing Your Draft

Once you have an outline to guide your writing, it is time to produce a first draft. The first draft is where you try out the organization you created in your outline and flesh out the ideas you identified to support your thesis. It is not the finished product. Just as a good movie begins with a rehearsal to review the script and try out techniques to produce the story, a good research paper begins with a draft in which you review material, try out ideas to see which ones will be most effective. A good draft can help you identify ways to express your information accurately and your thoughts persuasively.

Before you begin, it is a good idea to again consider the members of your audience: Who are they? What do they know? What style of writing and language will they find most interesting or persuasive?

Recognize that although members of your audience may all be of a similar background and educational level, they will not necessarily possess the same knowledge of the subject that you do. Ask yourself:

- How much of the information covered by your research is common knowledge? You want to provide sufficient explanation of unfamiliar concepts but, at the same time, not belabor the obvious.

- What questions will the reader have? Be sure you address all key questions that are essential to the reader's understanding of your subject.

- How will your reader react to your thesis? This is especially important in a persuasive paper where your goal is to have your readers accept your thesis.

- What kind of information is needed to move your reader to a better understanding of the subject or to agree with your assessment of it? The answers to this question will provide the topics for the paragraphs in the body of your paper.

- What do you want the reader to remember most? This will be the focus of your conclusion.

The answers to these questions will give you a sense of how much background you will need to include about your subject as well as the language and tone of writing that you should use to present it.

Introductions

Eventually (and with practice) all writers will develop their own strategy for writing the perfect introduction to an essay or research paper. Once you are comfortable with writing, you will probably find your own, but coming up with a good strategy can be tough for beginning writers. Here are some tips for perfecting your introduction:

First write your thesis. Your thesis should state the main idea in specific terms.

Preparing Your Draft

After you have a working thesis, tackle the body of your paper before you write the rest of the introduction. Each paragraph in the body should explore one specific topic that proves, or summarizes your thesis. Writing is a thinking process. Once you have worked your way through that process by writing the body of the paper, you will have an intimate understanding of how you are supporting your thesis. After you have written the body paragraphs, go back and rewrite your thesis to make it more specific and to connect it to the topics you addressed in the body paragraph.

Revise your introduction several times, saving each revision. Be sure your introduction previews the topics you are presenting in your paper. One way of doing this is to use keywords from the topic sentences in each paragraph to introduce, or preview, the topics in your introduction. This "preview" will give your reader a context for understanding how you will make your case.

Experiment by taking different approaches to your thesis with every revision you make. Play with the language in the introduction. Strike a new tone. Go back and compare versions. Then pick the one that works most effectively with the body of your essay.

Do not try to pack everything you want to say into your introduction. Just as your introduction should not be too short, it should also not be too long. Your introduction should be about the same length as any other paragraph in your essay. Let the content—what you have to say—dictate the length.

Starters for Introductions

- Interesting revelations about the subject
- A question that asks your audience to weigh the importance of the subject
- A relevant quotation or claim about the subject
- An anecdote that shows how your subject affects people's lives
- Important background or historical information about the subject
- A surprising piece of new information or interesting facts that your audience may not already know

Imperfect introductions come across as flat and lifeless and fail to engage the reader. They give the reader nothing that is new or interesting, or, worse, they use absolutes to present a world that does not exist. You should not use absolutes (words like always, never, everywhere, etc.) because the world is a big and diverse place; exceptions can always be found, and the only absolute that seems to be true is that absolutes rarely if ever exist. The minute you say everyone everywhere agrees, someone will pop up and insist that this is not so.

It is also a bad idea to open a paper with dictionary or encyclopedia definitions of terms that readers already know (it gives them no reason to continue) or by immediately referencing yourself (it gives the impression that you are writing a personal essay and that your paper is probably not research-based).

Phrases to Avoid in Your Introduction

- Avoid: Everyone agrees that …

    Instead say: Evidence indicates …

- Avoid: Everywhere in the world …/In all the world …

    Instead say: A common phenomenon is …
- Avoid: Every single …

    Instead say: Many …
- Avoid: All …

    Instead say: Most …
- Avoid: None … (or no one …)

    Instead say: Few …
- Avoid: Never …

    Instead say: Rarely …
- Avoid: Forever …/Always …

    Instead say: Many times …/Often …
- Avoid: Nowadays …

    Instead say: In recent times …
- Avoid: Some people may disagree but …/Not everyone agrees that …/Some may agree and others may disagree but …

    Instead say: Those who would argue the point contend that …
- Avoid: I think …/In my personal opinion …/It seems to me that …

    Instead say: It is clear that …/Clearly, …/ Obviously, …/
- Avoid: The dictionary defines …/According to Webster's, …

    Do not define common words, phrases, ideas, or concepts that your reader already knows. Begin with a strong statement about something new, surprising, or controversial about your topic.

The introduction sets the tone for what will follow and signals the reader about what to expect. It includes the thesis, the most important sentence in the paper, and it should be written in an interesting way that entices the audience to read on. It should not be too long, nor should it be too short; a half to three-quarters of a page is usually appropriate, but do not count lines. The length depends on the amount of explanation your thesis requires. The introduction has a lot of work to perform. Each component has to do its job for the introduction to be successful. Often the introduction is the most difficult paragraph to write. In your outline, you should have developed the elements that will go into the introduction, including an overview of your research, a good working thesis, and a tentative transition sentence leading to the topic in the next paragraph. The challenge is to present this information in an interesting order so that the ideas flow clearly from one to another.

Begin in a way that sets the tone and provide essential information for the type of paper you are producing:

- A simple summary might begin with a description of the topic.

- A history paper might take a narrative approach and present information chronologically in storytelling fashion.

- A persuasive paper might focus on recent debate about the topic or a curious or controversial interpretation of it and outline your position.

- Topics in which people or events have had a significant impact on the topic, such as a science report on a discovery or a history paper about the aftereffects of a war, might begin with an anecdote.

- A paper based on personal experiences, such as a scientific field survey, might begin with a detailed description of a site or setting.
- A paper that will advance a hypothesis might begin with a description of the question or problem the hypothesis is intended to address.
- Quotations can provide relevant openings for papers of all sorts. The key is to find one that is meaningful to your topic, to use it judiciously, and to cite it properly.

The opening phrases you use to begin the introduction should be followed by sentences that explicitly state the topic or purpose of the paper. This shows readers why they should read the paper, what they can expect to learn, and why they should read on.

After introducing the topic, it is time to present the thesis. Begin with the working thesis you developed for your outline. Can it be revised to make a stronger statement that better reflects the outcomes of your research? Since the thesis is the most important sentence in your essay, you should now give it careful thought and focus it around your topic. The thesis should:

- Identify the topic, main idea, or proposition that you intend to prove.
- Make a strong statement about the topic.
- Have a direct and logical relationship to the background material presented in the introduction.

■ Share the chief insight you gained from your research.

Your thesis should be introduced with a phrase that identifies your topic and shows your reader what you intend to do in the paper. If you are working on a classroom assignment, take your cues from what the assignment asks you to do. For instance, it if asks you to analyze something, use the word "analyze" when presenting your thesis. Simply appropriating words from an assignment, however, does not result in a perfect paper. You must then do what you say you will do; the introduction cannot promise readers one thing and deliver another. An analysis, for instance, must provide a close examination of the topic to inform readers about why things are the way they are. A discussion needs to focus on the merits of different sides of an issue. A persuasive paper must, in addition to advancing an opinion on the thesis, deliver compelling reasons for an audience to believe it. The example below shows an introduction that responds well to the assignment:

Assignment: The award-winning column, "The Death of Captain. Waskow" by war correspondent Ernie Pyle was one of the most widely published dispatches from the battlefront during World War II. However, John Rice, a correspondent for a competing news organization, criticized Pyle's style of journalism as "sentimental; they really say nothing about how the war was going at the time." Write a three-page analysis of the column that responds to this critique. Were Rice's comments justified? Does Pyle's report really say nothing about the progress of the war?

Strong introduction: In "The Death of Captain Waskow," a newspaper report filed from the battlefront during World War II, correspondent Ernie Pyle portrayed the experiences and emotions of battle-hardened soldiers— if not the facts of the campaign. Although the column has been criticized as "sentimental," it presented readers with a profound vision of war and its impact on those involved in it. Research into Pyle's personal history and an analysis of this column in particular reveals that Pyle's reporting style grew from the experience of someone who was there. He traveled with the army on the front line of battle, witnessed what the soldiers witnessed, and was thus able to present a much truer picture of the war than any "progress" report.

Weak introduction: Ernie Pyle, a newspaper correspondent in World War II, wrote a column called "The Death of Captain Waskow" that became one of the most widely published dispatches from the battlefront. However, John Rice, a correspondent for a competing news organization, criticized Pyle's style of journalism as "sentimental; they really say nothing about how the war was going at the time."

The assignment clearly asks the writer for an analysis. Note how the first introduction clearly states that the paper will provide analysis and introduces it by declaring Pyle's style of writing as "much truer" than the style his critic would have preferred.

The second introduction falls far short of what the assignment requests. It provides a summary, not an analysis. In restating the assignment, it shows little thought or originality. Worse, it plagiarizes the assignment by lifting information from it verbatim.

By restating the purpose of the assignment in your own words, such as the first introduction did above ("an analysis of this column in particular reveals that…"), you focus the intent of the paper and introduce your readers to what they can expect will follow.

Phrases for Introducing Thesis Statements

Analysis

- This *analysis* will provide …
- This paper *analyzes* the relationship between …
- This paper presents an *analysis* of …

Persuasion

- This paper will *argue* that …
- This topic *supports the argument that* …
- Research supports the *opinion* that …
- This paper supports the *opinion* that …

Findings

- An interpretation of the facts indicates …
- The results of this experiment show …
- The results of this research show …

Comparisons/Contrasts

- A *comparison* will show that …

- By *contrasting* the results, we see that …
- This paper examines the advantages and disadvantages of …

Definitions/Classifications

- This paper will provide a guide for *categorizing* the following: …
- This paper provides a *definition* of …
- This paper explores the meaning of …

Discussion

- This paper will *discuss* the implications of …
- A *discussion* of this topic reveals …
- The following *discussion* will focus on …

Description

- This report *describes* …
- This report will *illustrate* …
- This paper *provides an illustration* of …

Process/Experimentation

- This paper will identify *the reasons behind* …
- The results of the *experiment* show …
- The *process* revealed that …

Hypothesis

- This paper *theorizes* …

- This paper presents the *theory* that …
- In *theory,* this indicates that …

Paragraphs

The first sentence of your second paragraph should continue the transition from the end of your introduction to present your first topic. Often too, your first sentence will be your "topic sentence," the sentence that presents the topic, point, or argument that will be presented in the paragraph. The body of the paragraph should contain evidence, in the form of a discussion using quotations and examples, that supports or "proves" the topic. The final sentence of the paragraph should provide a transition to the third paragraph of the essay where the second topic will be presented.

The third and fourth paragraphs follow the same format as the second:

- Transition or topic sentence.
- Topic sentence (if not included in the first sentence).
- Supporting sentences including a discussion, quotations, or examples that support the topic sentence.
- Concluding sentence that transitions to the next paragraph.

The topic of each paragraph will be supported by the evidence you itemized in your outline. However, just as smooth transitions are required to connect your paragraphs, the sentences you write to present your evidence should possess transition words that connect ideas, focus attention on relevant information, and continue your discussion in a smooth and fluid manner. Transition words and phrases are important when you are suggesting or pointing out similarities between ideas, themes, opinions, or a set of facts. As with any perfect phrase, transition words within paragraphs should not be used gratuitously. Their meaning must conform to what you are trying to point out, as shown in the examples below:

- "Accordingly" or "in accordance with" indicates agreement.

  Example : Thomas Edison's experiments with electricity accordingly followed the theories of Benjamin Franklin, J. B. Priestly, and other pioneers of the previous century.

- "Analogous" or "analogously" contrasts different things or ideas that perform similar functions or make similar expressions.

  Example: A computer hard drive is *analogous* to a filing cabinet. Each stores important documents and data.

- "By comparison" or "comparatively" points out differences between things that otherwise are similar.

  Example: Roses require an alkaline soil. Azaleas, *by comparison*, prefer an acidic soil.

- "Corresponds to" or "correspondingly" indicates agreement or conformity.

  Example: The U.S. Constitution *corresponds to* England's Magna Carta in so far as both established a framework for a parliamentary system.

- "Equals," "equal to," or "equally" indicates the same degree or quality.

  Example: Vitamin C is *equally as* important as minerals in a well-balanced diet.

- "Equivalent" or "equivalently" indicates two ideas or things of approximately the same importance, size, or volume.

  Example: The notions of individual liberty and the right to a fair and speedy trial hold equivalent importance in the American legal system.

- "Common" or "in common with" indicates similar traits or qualities.

  Example: Darwin did not argue that humans were descended from the apes. Instead, he maintained that they shared a common ancestor.

- "In the same way," "in the same manner," "in the same vein," or "likewise," connects comparable traits, ideas, patterns, or activities.

  Example: John Roebling's suspension bridges in Brooklyn and Cincinnati were built in the same manner, with strong cables to support a metallic roadway.

  Example: Despite its delicate appearance, John Roebling's Brooklyn Bridge was built as a suspension bridge supported by strong cables. Cincinnati's Suspension Bridge, which Roebling also designed, was likewise supported by cables.

- "Kindred" indicates that two ideas or things are related by quality or character.

Example: Artists Vincent Van Gogh and Paul Gauguin are considered kindred spirits in the Impressionist Movement. "Like" or "as" are used to create a simile that builds reader understanding by comparing two dissimilar things. (Never use "like" as slang, as in: John Roebling was like a bridge designer.)

Examples: Her eyes shone like the sun. Her eyes were as bright as the sun.

- "Parallel" describes events, things, or ideas that occurred at the same time or that follow similar logic or patterns of behavior.

  Example: The original Ocktoberfests were held to occur in parallel with the autumn harvest.

- "Obviously" emphasizes a point that should be clear from the discussion.

  Example: Obviously, raccoons and other wildlife will attempt to find food and shelter in suburban areas as their woodland habitats disappear.

- "Similar" and "similarly" are used to make like comparisons.

  Example: Horses and ponies have similar physical characteristics although, as working farm animals, each was bred to perform different functions.

- "There is little debate" or "there is consensus" can be used to point out agreement.

  Example: There is little debate that the polar ice caps are melting. The question is whether global warming results from natural or human-made causes.

Other phrases that can be used to make transitions or connect ideas within paragraphs include:

- Use "alternately" or "alternatively" to suggest a different option.
- Use "antithesis" to indicate a direct opposite.
- Use "contradict" to indicate disagreement.
- Use "on the contrary" or "conversely" to indicate that something is different from what it seems.
- Use "dissimilar" to point out differences between two things.
- Use "diverse" to discuss differences among many things or people.
- Use "distinct" or "distinctly" to point out unique qualities.
- Use "inversely" to indicate an opposite idea.
- Use "it is debatable," "there is debate," or "there is disagreement" to suggest that there is more than one opinion about a subject.
- Use "rather" or "rather than" to point out an exception.
- Use "unique" or "uniquely" to indicate qualities that can be found nowhere else.
- Use "unlike" to indicate dissimilarities.
- Use "various" to indicate more than one kind.

Writing Topic Sentences

Remember, a sentence should express a complete thought, one thought per sentence—no more, no less. The longer and more convoluted your sentences become, the more likely you are to muddle the meaning, become repetitive, and bog yourself down in issues of grammar and construction. In your first draft, it is generally a good idea to keep those sentences relatively short and to the point. That way your ideas will be clearly stated. You will be able to clearly see the content that you have put down—what is there and what is missing—and add or subtract material as it is needed. The sentences will probably seem choppy and even simplistic. The purpose of a first draft is to ensure that you have recorded all the content you will need to make a convincing argument. You will work on smoothing and perfecting the language in subsequent drafts.

Adding Evidence

Transitioning from your topic sentence to the evidence that supports it can be problematic. It requires a transition, much like the transitions needed to move from one paragraph to the next. Choose phrases that connect the evidence directly to your topic sentence.

Phrases for Supporting Topic Sentences

- Consider this: (give an example or state evidence).
- If (identify one condition or event) then (identify the condition or event that will follow).
- It should go without saying that (point out an obvious condition).
- Note that (provide an example or observation).

- Take a look at (identify a condition; follow with an explanation of why you think it is important to the discussion).

- The authors had (identify their idea) in mind when they wrote "(use a quotation from their text that illustrates the idea)."

- The point is that (summarize the conclusion your reader should draw from your research).

- This becomes evident when (name the author) says that (paraphrase a quote from the author's writing).

- We see this in the following example: (provide an example of your own).

- (The author's name) offers the example of (summarize an example given by the author).

If an idea is controversial, you may need to add extra evidence to your paragraphs to persuade your reader. You may also find that a logical argument, one based solely on your evidence, is not persuasive enough and that you need to appeal to the reader's emotions.

Look for ways to incorporate your research without detracting from your argument.

Writing Transition Sentences

It is often difficult to write transitions that carry a reader clearly and logically on to the next paragraph (and the next topic) in an essay. Because you are moving from one topic to another, it is easy to simply stop one and start another. Great research papers, however, include good transitions that link the ideas in an interesting discussion so that readers can move smoothly and easily through your presentation. Close each of your paragraphs with an interesting transition sentence that introduces the topic coming up in the next paragraph.

Transition sentences should show a relationship between the two topics. Your transition will perform one of the following functions to introduce the new idea:

- Indicate that you will be expanding on information in a different way in the upcoming paragraph.
- Indicate that a comparison, contrast, or a cause-and-effect relationship between the topics will be discussed.
- Indicate that an example will be presented in the next paragraph.
- Indicate that a conclusion is coming up.

Transitions make a paper flow smoothly by showing readers how ideas and facts follow one another to point logically to a conclusion. They show relationships among the ideas, help the reader to understand, and, in a persuasive paper, lead the reader to the writer's conclusion.

Each paragraph should end with a transition sentence to conclude the discussion of the topic in the paragraph and gently introduce the reader to the topic that will be raised in the next paragraph. However, transitions also occur within paragraphs—from sentence to sentence—to add evidence, provide examples, or introduce a quotation.

The type of paper you are writing and the kinds of topics you are introducing will determine what type of transitional phrase you should use. Some useful phrases for transitions appear below. They are grouped according to the function they normally play in a paper. Transitions, however, are not simply phrases that are dropped into sentences. They are constructed to highlight meaning. Choose transitions that are appropriate to your topic and what you want the reader to do. Edit them to be sure they fit properly within the sentence to enhance the reader's understanding.

Transition Phrases for Comparisons

- We also see
- In addition to
- Notice that
- As well as
- Beside that,
- In comparison,
- Likewise,
- Once again,
- Similarly,
- Identically,
- For example,
- Comparatively, it can be seen that
- We see this when
- This corresponds to
- In other words,

- At the same time,
- By the same token,

Transition Phrases for Contrast

- By contrast,
- On the contrary,
- However,
- Nevertheless,
- An exception to this would be …
- Alongside that, we find …
- Besides,
- On one hand … on the other hand …
- [New information] presents an opposite view …
- Conversely, it could be argued …
- Other than that, we find that …
- We get an entirely different impression from …
- One point of differentiation is …
- Further investigation shows …
- Moreover,
- An exception can be found in the fact that …

Transition Phrases to Show a Process

- At the top we have … Near the bottom we have …
- Here we have … There we have …

- Continuing on,
- We progress to …
- Close up … In the distance …
- In addition to
- Next,
- Next up
- With this in mind,
- Moving in sequence,
- Proceeding sequentially,
- Moving to the next step,
- First, Second, Third, …
- 1 … 2 … 3 …
- Examining the activities in sequence,
- Sequentially,
- As a result,
- The end result is …
- Thus …
- To illustrate …
- Subsequently,
- One consequence of …
- If … then …
- It follows that …
- Hence,
- Therefore,
- This is chiefly due to …

- The next step …
- Later we find …

Phrases to Introduce Examples

- For example,
- For instance,
- Particularly,
- In particular,
- This includes,
- Specifically,
- To illustrate,
- One illustration is
- One example is
- This is illustrated by
- This can be seen when
- This is especially seen in
- This is chiefly seen when

Transition Phrases for Presenting Evidence

- Another point worthy of consideration is
- At the center of the issue is the notion that
- Before moving on, it should be pointed out that
- Another important point is
- Another idea worth considering is
- Consequently,
- Especially,

- Even more important,
- Getting beyond the obvious,
- In spite of all this,
- It follows that
- It is clear that
- More importantly,
- Most importantly,
- Therefore,

Conclusions

After the introduction, the conclusion is the most important part of the paper and, like the introduction, it is difficult to write. A good conclusion contains your parting thought—the idea that you most want your reader to remember. It should make a strong statement, one that resonates with your audience and ensures that any questions raised in your paper have been answered.

By the time you write the conclusion, you should have pointed out in the body of your essay why your topic is important to the reader, and you should have presented the reader with all your arguments. It is critical that you do not introduce new information or ideas in your conclusion. If you find that you have not yet made the arguments you wished to make or pointed out evidence you feel is crucial to your reader's understanding of your subject, you are not yet ready to write the conclusion; add another body paragraph before writing the conclusion.

The opening sentence of the conclusion should flow smoothly and logically from the transition sentence in the previous paragraph and lead the reader to reflect on your thesis. A good conclusion however, does not simply restate the thesis. You want to remind the reader of the thesis in your conclusion but reword it in a stronger fashion so that it is interesting and memorable to your audience. After reminding the reader of the thesis, the conclusion should then reflect on the topics in the body of the paper and summarize the key findings of your research. If you are writing a persuasive paper, it should summarize your key arguments and logically point your readers to the conclusion you wish them to reach.

Phrases for Conclusions

- All this requires us to (propose the next action or an alternative idea).

- Altogether, these findings indicate (point out the logical result).

- Finally, it is important to note (make your strongest point and follow with a recommendation).

- In conclusion (restate your thesis with greater emphasis).

- It is evident that (point out the logical result or obvious next action).

- In light of the evidence, (restate your thesis with greater emphasis).

- In short, (summarize your findings).

- It should be evident that we need to (propose the next action or an alternative idea).

- In summary, (summarize your findings).

- Looking ahead, it is obvious that (propose the next action or an alternative idea).

- My conclusion is (restate your thesis with greater emphasis).

- One last word must be said. (Follow with your opinion and propose a next action.)

- One concludes that (give your opinion).

- Overall, (summarize your findings).

- Reflecting on these facts, we can see that …

- The evidence presented above shows that (give your opinion).

- The reader can conclude (make the point you wish to make).

- These facts and observations support the idea that (offer a theory).

- This analysis reveals (state your findings).

- To conclude, (give an opinion based on the findings presented in the paper).

- To sum up this discussion, (summarize your findings).

- To summarize, (summarize your findings).

- We arrive at the following conclusion: (give an opinion based on the findings presented in the paper).

- We cannot ignore the fact that (state an important concern and follow with a call to action).

- We can postulate (give your opinion or offer a theory).

- We come to the conclusion that (give your opinion or offer a theory).
- We can now present the theory that (give your opinion or offer a theory).

Chapter 5

Revising Your Work

To paraphrase Yogi Berra, legendary manager of the New York Yankees, writing a research paper "isn't over until it's over." Allow plenty of time for the revision process. Revision allows you to perfect your prose, sharpen the vocabulary, and ensure that others' ideas are properly represented. As you revise, you will want to make sure that:

- Your introduction engages the reader and clearly presents a thesis that responds to your assignment.

- The body of your paper supports the thesis with laserlike focus.

- Your conclusion convinces your readers of the importance of what you wrote.

Revision often requires changing the structure of your work to achieve a more logical presentation, one that is more descriptive, or one that ensures you have met the parameters of your assignment. More than anything else, it requires that you check all the facts and quotations you used and ensure that you have cited them properly and have not plagiarized a writer.

Avoiding Plagiarism

Plagiarism, in its most basic definition, means representing other people's work and ideas as your own. Turning in a paper that you bought, borrowed, or stole from another student or downloaded from the Internet constitutes plagiarism. So does copying portions of text directly from your sources or from other texts you encountered in your research. It is a serious offense that, in school, can result in a range of penalties—from failing an assignment, earning a black mark on your academic record, to even being expelled. In the workplace, it can result in the loss of your professional reputation and the respect of your colleagues. It can affect your ability to earn promotions or find another job.

Plagiarism is not always deliberate. It can happen inadvertently when students do not understand how to properly present others' work within their own papers. Even when you go to great lengths to write a paper, plagiarism can occur if you fail to properly cite the words and ideas of others. Plagiarism can happen if:

- You borrow short phrases from your research sources but fail to cite the source.
- You paraphrase an idea from your research using your own words but you fail to cite the original author.
- You represent another students' work, even a short passage from it, as your own.
- You turn in a paper that you previously submitted as an assignment for another class. (Yes! It is possible to plagiarize yourself.)

More often than not, plagiarism results from a writer's failure to properly paraphrase or summarize another's work or to correctly cite quoted material. Therefore, it is important to understand how to avoid plagiarism and to incorporate strategies for avoiding it in your writing routine. Plagiarism is easy to avoid if you have properly documented your research (see the section in Chapter 2, "Documenting Your Research") and if you follow the guidelines of an editorial stylebook, such as those published by the Modern Language Association (MLA) or the American Psychological Association (APA), to properly cite the research sources you documented.

Protecting Yourself against Plagiarism

Plagiarism is not just something that a writer can do; it is also something that can happen to a writer. In addition to taking care not to plagiarize others, you will want to protect your own work against plagiarism by others. And, if your instructor should call upon you to prove that your work is your own, you want to be in a position to do so. Things you can do to protect yourself include:

- Print and keep drafts of your work so that you can produce them if you are called upon to show the steps you took along the way.
- Store your files on memory sticks or flash drives when using public computers.
- When you have finished working on a public computer, close all your files and reboot the computer. Be sure to collect all devices and notes you brought with you. Leave nothing behind.

■ If a public computer reboots while you are working at it, be sure to reopen any files that were automatically saved and delete them properly. This ensures that anyone who uses the computer after you cannot retrieve those files.

Choosing a Documentation Style

"Style" refers to the way you present information and write what you have to say. Style guides prescribe conventions for writing and documenting your sources. Numerous styles abound. The three main styles are:

1. MLA (Modern Language Association) style: used by the vast majority of high schools, colleges, and in literature, linguistics, and the humanities programs.
2. APA (American Psychological Association) style: widely used in the scientific community.
3. *Chicago Manual of Style*: typically used in books, magazines, corporate publications, and other popular outlets.

Styles aim to bring consistency to the way in which information is presented. They are designed to promote intellectual integrity and protect writers against plagiarism by specifying the ways in which information should be reported, quoted, paraphrased, and summarized.

In the vast majority of cases, students producing research papers will follow MLA style, although APA style is also used in the academic community. MLA style is widely used among high schools and in undergraduate courses at the college and university level. Straightforward and easy to master, MLA style was developed more than 50 years ago and is also widely used by collegiate presses and scholarly publications.

Upper-level and graduate-level science courses, and other disciplines that present findings in case studies, whitepapers, and reports, typically follow APA style. Your selection of style, however, should always be based upon what your teacher or professor assigns.

Mastering the Basics

In this book, we review some of the basics of each style and provide a sample paper to illustrate basic MLA format. Students and serious researchers are advised to refer to the style guide of the association whose style they will follow.

Volumes have been published on the rules and recommendations of both styles. The MLA publishes the widely used *MLA Handbook for Writers of Research*, as well as the *MLA Style Manual and Guide to Scholarly Publishing* which offers more detailed guidance for graduate theses, dissertations, and papers to be published in journals. The APA offers a variety of style guides, including *Mastering APA Style* and the *Publication Manual of the American Psychological Association*, as well as extensive information online, including a narrated tutorial, at www.apastyle.org.

Numerous online writing labs (OWLs) sponsored by university writing programs, such as the ones below, also provide extensive resources to help you brainstorm, outline, and write papers, as well as avoid plagiarism:

Purdue University http://owl.english.purdue.edu/

University of Wisconsin http://writing.wisc.edu/Handbook/ Documentation.html

University of North Carolina www.unc.edu/depts/wcweb/

Basic Formatting Guidelines

Some common rules apply no matter which style you follow:

1. Never submit a handwritten paper.
2. Papers should be typewritten on plain white 8 $\frac{1}{2}$– × 11-inch paper.
3. Use 1-inch margins on all sides.
4. Double-space the paper.
5. Text should be justified flush left, leaving the right-hand margin ragged.
6. Create a header to run consecutively on all pages, flush right, one-half inch from the top of the page. (The contents of the header will vary based on which style you follow.)
7. Use quotation marks around the titles of articles and underline or italicize the titles of books and other long works.
8. Avoid using all caps, underlining, or italics for emphasis.

Other formatting considerations are particular to the style you choose.

MLA Formatting Basics

1. Include your name, your instructor's name, the name of the course, and the date in the top left corner of the first page.
2. Use a 12-point font that will be easy to read, such as Times New Roman or Arial.
3. Use 1-inch margins for all sides of the paper—top and bottom, right and left.

4. Create a header with your last name and the page number to appear in the upper right-hand corner of all other pages that follow the first page.

5. Avoid separate title pages. Instead insert one blank line (no more) beneath the date and center the title.

6. Never add blank lines or extra white space to the paper. Your teacher will suspect you are wasting space to fill a page requirement.

7. Type the title in title case, capitalizing the initial letter of keywords.

8. Center the title two lines under the header and just above the first line of text on the first page.

9. Insert one blank line (no more) beneath the title and begin writing. Do not include extra white space above or below the title.

10. Do not boldface or italicize the title and do not use special fonts. The title should be the same size and typeface as the rest of the paper.

11. Justify your text flush left.

12. Indent quoted excerpts by five spaces on the left and right-hand sides of the quoted text.

13. Double space the entire essay including header information, your works cited page, and quoted excerpts.

14. Be sure your works cited entries are formatted in the same style and size text as your paper. This is something you should especially watch if you used a citation generator; most produce the citation in their own fonts.

15. Indent paragraphs five spaces, or $\frac{1}{2}$ inch; do not add extra white space between paragraphs.

16. Use one space after punctuation.

APA Formatting Basics

APA style was developed by social and behavioral scientists to govern the structure and presentation of scientific writing. Unlike MLA style, APA style calls for a separate title page and unique sections within the paper. The sections include:

1. The title page
2. An abstract summarizing the paper
3. An introduction
4. A description of the scientific methodology the researcher used
5. A summary of the results
6. A discussion of the issues
7. References
8. Appendices

The references page is equivalent to the MLA's works cited page. It is a list of the sources cited within the paper. As in MLA style, the referenced works should be alphabetized by author's last name, listed separately, and formatted with hanging indents. Unlike MLA style, APA style makes liberal use of headings and uses five different levels of headings, each with unique formatting requirements. Check the APA Web site or style guide for details. When using APA style, remember to:

1. Use a serif typeface, such as Times New Roman, for the text.
2. Use a sans serif typeface, such as Arial, for headings.
3. Create separate pages for the title page, abstract, the beginning of the text, references, and each appendix, figure, illustration, or table you use in the paper.
4. Use captions with charts, tables, figures, illustrations, and other graphics.

Quotations/Citations

Any direct quotations or specific information you use from your sources must be attributed to your source, either by mentioning the author in the text or through an in-text citation. Quotation marks must appear around any words or phrases that appear exactly as they did in the original document.

If you mention the author to introduce the quotation, you will need to follow it with a page citation to ensure that you avoid plagiarism, as shown in the example below:

Anne-Marie Minnow explained the importance of the Hadron supercollider as "an innovation that will advance scientific understanding by light-years." (127)

If you do not include the author's name in your text, you will need to incorporate the author's last name in front of the page number in the citation, as shown in the example below:

The Hadron supercollider promises to be "an innovation that will advance scientific understanding by light-years." (Minnow 127)

Note that the first example is a narrative reference in which the writer mentions the full name of the author in order to introduce, or set up, the quotation. In the second example, the citation follows the quotation to identify who the author is. In both cases, it is clear the words being quoted belong to Minnow and, in addition to using in-text citations like those shown above, you will need to cite the source on your works cited page.

When to Quote

- Use quotations that establish examples, support your topics, and advance your argument. Do not quote for the sake of quoting.

- Use quotation marks around the exact words of the writer or speaker you are quoting.

- Note the name of the author, or speaker, of the quotation when you introduce the quotation or in a citation.

- If you are using a quotation that your source used, the citation process becomes a bit tricky. Be aware that you must always cite the author of the book you used. If that author quoted someone else and you want to use the other person's quote, you must handle it in your writing. The quotation should be attributed to the person who said it while the citation must refer to the source in which you found the quote. In the following example, for instance, the quotation belongs to Sir Isaac Newton but it came from a book by an author named Lindley.

  As Isaac Newton once said "I can calculate the motion of heavenly bodies, but not the madness of people." (Lindley 96)

- Be judicious with your quotations. You want to quote enough to enhance your audience's understanding of what you have to say but not so much that your teacher suspects you are letting the quotations write the paper for you. Look for ways to paraphrase and put ideas into your own words and be prepared to elaborate and provide examples for the material you quote.

Never change the wording of a direct quotation. Instead, use ellipses and brackets to clarify the meaning. Ellipses are three periods (…) that are inserted when you shorten a quotation by eliminating words that are not required for the reader's understanding. Brackets ([ ]) are used to add words or change letters within quotations to make them grammatically correct when they are removed from their original context. In the following example, brackets were inserted with lowercase letters when uppercase had been used, and the ellipsis is used to indicate that some words were omitted:

According to Longinus, "[T]he effect of elevated language upon an audience is not persuasion but transport… imposing speech, with the spell it throws over us, prevails over that which aims at persuasion and gratification."

All quotations, as well as any unique ideas offered by an author, should be cited. The information included in the citation and the correct way of formatting it will be dictated by the style that you use. If you use an online automatic citation generator, it will prompt you for the required information after you select a style. There are also numerous other online resources (Purdue University's online writing lab—OWL is a great one, http:// owl.english.purdue.edu/) and print style guides that will show you the correct format for citations ranging from books to television documentaries to Web sites to personal interviews.

It is also important to introduce the quotations that you use. Never let a quotation stand alone. Introduce it with a phrase that identifies who said it, as in *U.S. President Barrack Obama said…* or *Mark Twain once wrote…*

What to Cite

- Exact wording in phrases, full sentences, or passages found in magazine and newspaper articles, books, journals, reports, advertising, and other print sources.

- Exact wording in phrases, full sentences, or passages from TV and radio broadcasts, interviews, speeches, panel discussions, conversations, and other oral communications.

- Summaries of the original ideas, findings, or conclusions of others that you found in your research.

- Photographs, drawings and illustrations, charts and graphs, diagrams and schematics, and other pictorial images.

What Not to Cite

- Your own ideas, words, experiences, conclusions, or findings.

- Common knowledge, things that are generally well-known and widely reported across numerous sources. Use your best judgment as to what is common knowledge. If it is something you have heard before from other sources or studied in school, it is probably common knowledge. However, if you are in doubt, cite it. It is always better to cite something that need not be cited than to omit a citation that you truly needed.

  Example: U.S. Presidential elections are held every four years.

- Widely held beliefs.

  Example: Exercise and a healthy diet help to control body weight.

- Traditional and well-known stories, tales, myths, and legends from indeterminate authors.

  Example: The story goes on and on, like those of the Arabian Nights.

- Current and historical events that are or were reported as news.

  Example: The attack on Pearl Harbor in 1941 prompted the United States to enter World War II.

Phrases to Introduce Quotations

- The writer explains it by saying, "…"
- According to [author/speaker's name], "…"
- The author writes, "…"
- The author says, "…"
- [Author's name] says, "…"
- [Author's name] writes, "…"
- [Author's name] summarizes this by saying, "…"
- [Author's name] was correct when he/she said, "…"
- [Author's name] was incorrect when he/she said, "…"
- [Author's name] points out that, "…"

Summaries/Paraphrases

Paraphrasing and summarizing are ways of discussing the work and ideas of others without quoting them directly. We summarize a discussion or reading to make it more succinct so that it can fit more neatly into our own discussion. We paraphrase a discussion in order to make it clearer or more relevant to our thesis and our audience. For all practical purposes, summary and paraphrase mean the same thing—using your own words to represent another's ideas. It is equally as important to cite authors whose ideas you summarize or paraphrase as it is to cite those you quote.

Tips for Summarizing and Paraphrasing

Following are some tips you can apply when you are summarizing or paraphrasing:

- Whenever you summarize or paraphrase, write your understanding of the text you are summarizing. Avoid looking at the text as you do. This will help ensure that you do not inadvertently borrow the writer's phrases. When you have finished, compare what you have written to the author's words and correct any inaccuracies, again using your own words. If you used significant words or phrases from the original text, be sure to enclose them in quotation marks.

- As you incorporate your summaries and paraphrases into your paper, cite them as carefully as you cite quoted material.

- Be especially cautious when using word processing tools like Microsoft Word's AutoSummarize. AutoSummarize shortens a page of text, highlighting key points and phrases that can be inserted into a research paper. Instructors are aware of these features, and many do not consider them legitimate. It is arguable, after all, whether this is you or the word processor doing the job. If you do use this feature, be sure that you edit the autosummary to quote the words and phrases that the word processor extracted from the original and be sure that you cite the source.

- Whenever you summarize or paraphrase, begin with a signal phrase to introduce the material. Be sure to cite the material as you would cite a quotation.

Phrases to Introduce Summaries

- In general,
- In short,
- In brief,
- In summary,
- To summarize,
- To restate,
- Generally,
- Generally speaking,
- Typically,
- Usually,
- As usual,
- As a general rule,
- As a rule,
- In most circumstances,
- In essence,
- In other words,
- On the whole,

Phrases to Introduce Paraphrases

- The author tells us that
- According to the author,
- The author writes …

- The author says that …
- The author states that …

Bibliographies/Works Cited

Bibliographies and works cited are not the same. Bibliographies include all the sources you consulted in your research whether or not you cite or mention them at all in your paper. Your works cited should include only the sources that you cite. Instructors will ask for bibliographies when they want to review all the research you conducted to prepare for the paper.

Do not try to "wow" your instructor with a long bibliography when your instructor requests only a works cited page. It is tempting, after doing a lot of work to research a paper, to try to include summaries on each source as you write your paper so that your instructor appreciates how much work you did. That is a trap you want to avoid. MLA style, the one that is most commonly followed in high schools and university writing courses, dictates that you include only the works you actually cited in your paper—not all those that you used.

Assembling Bibliographies and Works Cited

- If your assignment calls for a bibliography, list all the sources you consulted in your research.
- If your assignment calls for a works cited or references page, include only the sources you quote, summarize, paraphrase, or mention in your paper.
- If your works cited page includes a source that you did not cite in your paper, delete it.

- All in-text citations that you used at the end of quotations, summaries, and paraphrases to credit others for their ideas, words, and work must be accompanied by a cited reference in the bibliography or works cited. These references must include specific information about the source so that your readers can identify precisely where the information came from. The citation entries on a works cited page typically include the author's name, the name of the article, the name of the publication, the name of the publisher (for books), where it was published (for books), and when it was published.

The good news is that you do not have to memorize all the many ways the works cited entries should be written. Numerous helpful style guides are available to show you the information that should be included, in what order it should appear, and how to format it. The format often differs according to the style guide you are using. The Modern Language Association (MLA) follows a particular style that is a bit different from APA (American Psychological Association) style, and both are somewhat different from the *Chicago Manual of Style* (CMS). Always ask your teacher which style you should use.

Once you know the style you should follow, you can use one of the many valuable online tools that are available to help you generate citations. They can be found on Web sites like Citation Machine (http://citationmachine.net/), Easybib (www.easybib.com/), BibMe (www.bibme.org/), and Knight Cite from the Heckman Library at Michigan's Calvin College (www.calvin.edu/library/knightcite/). These sites include fill-in-the-blank forms that will automatically generate correctly formatted citations. All you need to do is select the style you are assigned to follow and fill in the correct information. The citation generator will produce a citation that you can copy and paste into your works cited page. (See Figure 5.1.)

Citation generators allow you to select the academic style your teacher prefers. They then prompt you for the information needed for the citation and automatically generate a properly

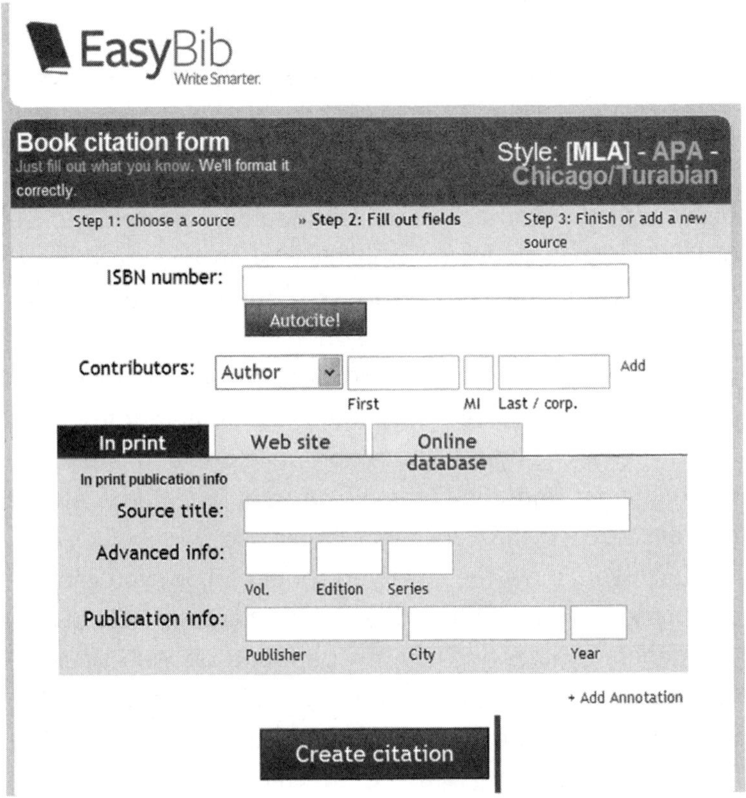

Figure 5.1 Citation generators like EasyBib automatically format citations from information you enter into an online form.

formatted citation. All you need to do is copy the text from the generator's window and paste it, alphabetically by the initial word, into your works cited page.

Be sure you select the required style to receive the citation in the correct style for your paper. The program will present a form that prompts you for the required information. Be sure to provide all of the information requested in the form. You might want to keep the citation Web site open in a separate window as you do your research and enter the information as you begin to cite references. After the citation is generated, you can copy and paste the in-text and works cited citations into your paper.

Citation generators are not perfect, however. They do not think for themselves and can work only with the information you enter into them. They also cannot format the full bibliographic page for you.

How to Generate Citations

- Be sure CAPS LOCK is turned off.

- Spell all words correctly.

- Give special attention to names. Make sure that the names of authors and titles on your works cited page are spelled correctly and consistently throughout your paper. Avoid abbreviations and short-cuts. Do not, for instance, enter Journal of Am. Studies in the citation generator if the title is Journal of American Studies.

- Be sure punctuation in your entries accurately conforms to the punctuation in the titles and subtitles. Be attentive to colons, dashes, and ampersands in titles and subtitles.

- Make sure that all the required information is included.

- After you have pasted the entry into your works cited page, be sure to format it as you did the rest of your paper.

- Proofread every entry to ensure that it is complete and correct.

- When creating your works cited page, be sure to center the heading "Works Cited" at the top of the page and alphabetize the citations according to the authors' last names.

Avoiding Bias

Readers are particularly sensitive to the use of words and phrases that express bias toward groups or individuals. Unfortunately, the effort to eliminate bias from language has often been attacked in the popular press as "politically correct." In fact, it is not political at all. It is on the one hand a simple matter of courtesy, being sensitive to the feelings of others as you would want others to be sensitive to you. On the other, it is inspired in academic communities by the need for neutral investigation and scientific integrity. Bias, whether it is intentional or inadvertent, destroys objectivity. In science, it produces unreliable results.

Both the MLA and the APA have responded to these concerns with guidelines that encourage writers to reduce bias by avoiding words and expressions that convey it. They advise you to pay close attention to language and apply rules of courtesy and common sense as you edit your work. For example,

1. Avoid using street language and slang appellations, especially in reference to people. Instead, provide specific demographic information such as age and national origin.

2. Do not use your own race or cultural heritage as the standard against which individuals, groups, survey results, or field observations are evaluated.

3. Strike adjectives that convey value judgments (such as superior, inferior, beautiful, pretty, attractive, ugly, plain, mediocre, intelligent, average, slow, etc.) from your descriptions.

When writing about racial, gender, cultural, physical, psychological, or religious issues, take care to avoid stereotypical language. Be descriptive and precise and avoid generic labels.

Editing to Eliminate Bias

Questionable Expressions	Preferred Expressions
The disabled	Persons with disabilities
Handicap	Disability
Birth defect	Birth impairment
The mentally ill	Persons with mental illness
The mentally disturbed	Persons possessing psychiatric disabilities
Homosexual	Lesbian, or gay man. Male-male, or female-female
Heterosexual behavior	Male-female behavior
Homosexual behavior	Male-male behavior, or female-female behavior

The opposite sex	Women, men, males, females
Sex	Gender
Sexual intercourse	Sexual activity
Bisexual	Bisexual persons
Gay (alone)	Gay male, gay woman

The APA publishes extensive guidelines advising researchers to examine and edit their surveys and questionnaires, as well as their writing of scientific research papers, to avoid bias. Writers in all disciplines would be well-advised to consider these guidelines as they write. They include:

1. Focus on the people and their accomplishments—not on their race, disability, or gender.
2. Be specific in your descriptions of the situations faced by the people you are discussing.
3. Avoid labels that stereotype behaviors, symptoms, or social conditions.
4. Do not use the word "handicap" to describe a disability. Instead, the word should be used to describe the obstacles that limit the activities of persons with disabilities.
5. Avoid phrasing that implies that a subject is performing in a submissive way or is being acted upon by others. This can often be accomplished by avoiding the passive voice. "Thirteen students took the test," for instance, is preferable to "The test was given to 13 students."

Specificity not only helps you avoid bias in writing, but it adds information that is valuable to your audience. Consider, for instance, the following sentence:

We surveyed 200 people between the ages of 25 and 40.

It offers some information but, other than providing an age range, gives readers no clear understanding of the demographics of the survey. Compare it to the sentence below.

We surveyed 200 people between the ages of 25 and 40, including 100 men, of whom 35 were black; 35 Caucasian; and 30 Hispanic; and 100 women of the same ethnic distribution.

The APA advises that sensitivity should be applied to the information gathering process as well. Using inappropriate or ambiguous language during an interview, in a survey, or on a questionnaire, is likely to have a negative impact on your subjects and, thus, your results.

Chapter 6

Polishing Your Writing

E diting is the process of fine-tuning words and phrases to perfect your research paper. Like revision, it requires you to rewrite, but editing means making small or subtle changes to improve language and usage, rather than making substantial changes in the content. Editing involves finding ways to improve your research paper by stating things more clearly and descriptively, by deleting extraneous material, by calling on your vocabulary and by changing word choices to avoid repetition. It also means catching and correcting run-on and incomplete sentences, as well as other errors in grammar, punctuation, and spelling.

It is often a good idea to walk away from a draft after you have revised it but before you begin editing to improve your prose. Save the file and let it rest. Go on to other assignments. Call a friend. Go out for a cup of coffee. Watch a favorite television program. Let your mind move away from your topic. When you come back to it, you will find that you are better able to revise, edit, and improve your work.

Why not revise immediately? Because immediately after composing a draft, your mind is still engaged in your work. It remembers what you wanted to say, or thought you said; your eyes tend to overlook omissions and errors as you proofread. You are much more likely to catch them when you read your work with a fresh eye.

Another strategy for improving your work is to read it aloud to yourself or work with a friend and have him or her read the paper back to you. Often, we hear mistakes that our eyes overlook. Writers remember what they intended to say and, often in their haste to edit, proofread, and finish the paper, they consider the meaning on their mind rather than what their readers are likely to perceive. Hearing sentences spoken aloud, as if they were said to you in conversation, gives you an opportunity to perceive the meaning as a reader would.

As you read, listen for words and phrases that are often repeated, discussions that stray from your point, explanations that are not clear, words that are missing, and sentences that sound awkward, incomplete, or run on. Be sure every sentence in each of your paragraphs supports the topic sentence. If you find that you introduced a new topic in the middle of a paragraph, mark the spot. Then ask yourself if the new topic is germane to your thesis. If the answer is yes, create a new paragraph to discuss the new material. If the answer is no, the material probably distracts from your thesis and should be deleted.

Vocabulary

Words are the building blocks of perfect papers. They lay the foundation for all that will follow and deserve to be used well in sentences. Good use of words displays your intelligence and your attention to detail.

The key to demonstrating a strong vocabulary in the papers you write is to use words clearly and accurately, not to impress your teacher by peppering your paper with synonyms you found in the thesaurus. English novelist George Eliot stated: "The finest language is mostly made up of simple unimposing words." Be specific and be correct.

Using precise words to express precise meanings that point your readers in the direction you wish them to go minimizes the risk that they will misunderstand what you are saying. If you turn to the thesaurus to avoid repeating the same word too often in a paper, be sure to follow up by using a dictionary to check the meaning of the new word so that you are sure to use it correctly.

While you do want to demonstrate a good vocabulary to your instructor, you want to use words that your reader will understand. The risk in relying heavily on your thesaurus is twofold:

1. You may change the meaning by choosing words that are close to—but not right on—the meaning you want. For instance, synonyms that the thesaurus gives for the word "maneuver" include artifice, contrivance, curveball, device, dodge, fancy footwork, feint, finesse, intrigue, jig, machination, manipulation, measure, play, plot, ruse, scheme, shenanigans, shuffle, step, stunt, subterfuge, and trick. However, you would want to use none of these if you were discussing military Allied maneuvers in France during World War II. Other synonyms that the thesaurus gives for maneuver would be more appropriate: action, movement, plan, or stratagem.

2. You overwhelm your reader with fancy words. If your reader has no idea what the word means, even if it does mean exactly what you want to say, you have defeated your purpose.

Use your thesaurus, but let the dictionary be your guide; check the meaning of the word you select to ensure that its definition not only fits your purpose but also that you are using it correctly in your sentence. Avoid using words and phrases that seem formal, stilted, old-fashioned, or vague and replace them with words and phrases that are specific, to the point, and familiar to your reader.

Better yet, make it a point to learn how to use new words. One of the best ways is to look up unfamiliar words you encounter in your reading and research. Note how the authors use them and make a point of using them yourself in your speech and writing.

You can also subscribe to electronic newsletters that will e-mail you new words, their definitions, and even their pronunciations each day. Dictionary.com's (www.dictionary.reference. com/) Word of the Day is ideal for students who want to build upon a basic vocabulary. Wordsmith.org (www.word smith.org/) offers a daily newsletter for academics, professionals, and other word lovers who want to take their well-informed vocabularies to a higher level.

To subscribe to Dictionary.com's Word of the Day, send a blank e-mail message to: join-wordoftheday@lists.lexico.com. Visit www.wordsmith.org to subscribe to the A.Word.A.Day (AWAD) newsletter.

Checking Your Usage

Short words and commonly used words and expressions, as well as big ones, can cause problems in writing if they are used incorrectly. Names destroy credibility when they are misspelled or misidentified, and even quotations can add to confusion if they are not introduced properly. Below are some simple rules for usage that can help you avoid these problems.

Basic Rules of Usage

- *People, places, and things.* Use *who* for people and *that* for places, ideas, and things.

  Examples: The senator who spoke, the woman who runs the coffee shop; the countries that are battling, the thought that one would do such a thing; the color that matches the paint on the walls.

- *Numbers and volumes of things.* Use *many* or *few* for things you count. Use *more* or *less* for things you pour or perceive.

  Examples: Many fish in the sea, many times, few circumstances that I can recall.

  Examples: Less food, less use of …, more sunlight, more sympathy.

- *Time.* Do not use vague and colloquial expressions like *nowadays, these days, long ago, throughout history, since the dawn of time, once upon a time,* or *as long as anyone can remember.* They do not give readers a specific frame of reference. Instead, be specific.

  Examples: Middle Ages, the last century, in the last few years (months, or weeks), currently or presently (for ongoing conditions).

- *Assumed knowledge and universal agreement.* Do not use phrases such as *everyone knows* (or *agrees*) *that …, No one can argue that …,* or *Anyone can tell you that …* or any other expression that assumes universal understanding. It is a sure bet that someone, somewhere, does not know it, will argue it, or cannot tell you a thing about it. Just state the fact.

- *Contractions.* Avoid contractions—those truncated expressions that use an apostrophe to combine two words. They introduce errors when you leave out an apostrophe or inadvertently type a "sound-alike." Many instructors also consider the use of contractions inappropriate and informal for writing assignments.

  - Instead of *it's,* use *it is* to avoid the erroneous use of *its.*

  - Instead of *could've,* use *could have* so you do not inadvertently write the grammatically incorrect *could of.*

  - Instead of *they're,* use *they are* to ensure that you do not make the mistake of typing a sound-alike such as *their* or *there.*

- *Quotations.* Do not let a quotation stand on its own without referencing who said it. Instead, use a phrase that references the author and offers enough explanation to give context to the quotation. Consider the sentence, *"Averting that threat has become the most urgent problem of our time."* The reader does not know who said it or what threat the person was describing. Using an introduction with the quotation corrects the problem: *Albert Einstein warned that his theory of relativity could be used to build devastating weapons, stating, "Averting that threat has become the most urgent problem of our time."*

- *Then/than.* These words are not interchangeable. Use *then* to indicate a sequential order of people/things/events or a time in the past. Use *than* when making a comparison.

Examples: The experiment seemed to go awry; *then* it followed the expected pattern. More ducks *than* falcons are found in the Carolina intercoastal.

- *Names.* Be sure they are spelled correctly and used properly. Check the spelling of all names of people, places, and things, letter-for-letter against the spellings given in your research sources. Always use first and last names, plus the person's title or a phrase identifying the person the first time you mention the individual in your paper.

  Example: *Dr. Miles AuGratin, a psychologist with the River City Clinical Research Lab, postulates this theory.*

  After the first reference, use the person's last name only. Never refer to a person only by his or her first name.

- *Single sentence paragraphs.* You see them in newspaper articles and Internet text all the time, but it is best to avoid them in a formal research paper. Teachers tend to frown on single sentence paragraphs; they want to see expanded arguments that include more of your reasoning. Develop any single sentence into the topic sentence of a paragraph and support it with research to expand the idea.

- *Starting a sentence with a conjunction.* Conjunctions are connecting words like "and" and "but" which join independent thoughts, often full sentences. Many teachers discourage students from starting sentences with them.

- *Ending a sentence with a preposition.* For the sake of clarity, it is a good idea to avoid ending a sentence with a preposition and, instead, complete the thought.

Example: He said he planned *to*.

The sentence above is unclear. It assumes the reader knows what "he" planned to do. His intent becomes clear when the sentence is written to complete the thought and avoid the preposition at the end.

Example: He said he planned to turn in the assignment on time.

Avoiding the "I" Trap

A good rule to keep in mind as you write a research paper is, "It is not all about me." Many writers defend their thesis by adding "I think" to every conclusion they make about it. That is not a good idea. Many teachers in high school, and especially in college, frown on students using first person references (like I, me, my, we, or our) in a research paper. Others find it acceptable, although usually on a limited basis or when the assignment specifically calls for you to do a first-person description or narrative. Many students freeze, however, when it comes to putting down their ideas without writing "I think" to introduce them. That is no reason to let writer's block set it—and there is an easy way to avoid making the paper all about you.

The advice here is: Go ahead and write *I think*. Why? Because you can write anything in a first draft. The draft is there to get you started. You will go back and revise it anyway. Rewrite it to your heart's content. So keep those ideas flowing. Use "I think" and "in my opinion" all you want. Just concentrate on getting your ideas down on paper or screen. When you have finished your draft, go back and delete all the "I thinks" and "In my opinions" that you find.

Just drop them. You will find that most sentences will be able to stand up on their own (or with very little rewrite) without you inserting yourself to support them. Your reader's attention will be focused where you want it—on the ideas, not on you.

It is not a capital offense to refer to yourself in an essay. After all, you are the writer. Be aware, however, that many high school teachers and most college professors frown on it; in the professional world, it is almost never done. Ideas should stand on their own. A paper full of *I think*s and *In my opinion*s leaves the impression that you are not confident in your research. In the examples below, notice how much more authoritative the second example is than the first.

1. I think that science has not yet uncovered evidence that intelligent life exists anywhere in the universe except on Earth.

2. Science has yet to uncover evidence that intelligent life exists anywhere in the universe except on Earth.

Polishing the Prose

Many times in editing, you will find that your topics are not well-developed. You may have to "wordsmith" by subtracting some words, adding others, changing the language, and rewriting what is already on paper in order to provide an even flow of language as well as ideas. This can be a difficult task. After working so hard to write a paper, it is painful to have to cut or change what you already wrote, but your paper gets closer to perfection every time you do.

In addition to presenting ideas and information in a clear and organized fashion, you should edit your grammar, punctuation, word usage, and spelling. The list below offers guidance on editing for some of the most common problems in writing. It does not address the many things that can go wrong grammatically. There are literally hundreds of style guides and grammar handbooks on the market. Invest in one and use it to look up issues such as when and how to use colons or whether you should use "that" or "which" to introduce a clause.

- *You find repetition.* Consecutive sentences that begin with the same word should be changed. Similarly, if the same words are repeated over and over again in a paragraph, you should find meaningful synonyms or names to replace them. Note how the original paragraph below was edited to avoid repetition.

  Original version: In any sentence, the verb signifies the action. The subject can perform the action. The subject can also be acted upon by the verb. The active tense is when the subject performs the action. The passive tense is when the subject is acted upon.

  Edited version: Verbs signify action that can be active or passive. The tense is active when the subject performs the action. It is passive when the subject is acted upon.

- *Ideas become belabored.* Belaboring an idea means saying the same thing over and over but using different words to say it. Say what you have to say, and then stop. In the examples below, notice how the edited version is much more to the point:

Belabored text: Walking is a skill that most children acquire by the age of two. It involves the development of their motor skills, and they are typically able to do it by their second birthday.

Edited text: Most children, by the time they are two years old, have developed the motor skills needed to walk.

- *The prose is too pretty.* Flowery words, alliteration, puns, pointless rhymes, and inappropriate metaphors and similes can cause trouble. They may sound cute, or even lovely, but they do not belong in a research paper if they have nothing to do with your topic. Remember, a research paper is not a poem or an ode to your mother's flower garden. Stay close to your findings and avoid descriptions like "mountainous men moving mysteriously in the mist."

- *Sentences run on or are overly wordy.* Reading your paper aloud to yourself or another helps to identify such problems. If you have spoken a mouthful before getting to a period, break apart the ideas into separate sentences. Notice how a personal observation ("it is not surprising") and redundant phrases ("in that era" and "during that time") were removed and edits were made to correct the sentence below:

Example: It is not surprising that discussions of the historical contexts of novels written in that era focus on the revolution at the expense of the intensity of attention given during that time to the maritime exploration and expansion that fed the emerging Industrial Revolution.

Corrected: Discussions of the historical events that occurred in the era when the novels were written tend to focus on the revolution and not the explorations and colonial expansion that fed the Industrial Revolution.

■ *Sentences are incomplete.* Just as some sentences run on too long, others do not run far enough. Incomplete sentences lack key elements needed for understanding. The sentence below is incomplete; it does not tell readers how the metaphors were used.

The way the metaphors are in this story,

The sentence can be rewritten with additional material to complete the thought and promote readers' understanding.

Metaphors are used in this story to build a visual awareness of the life of a soldier in Afghanistan.

■ *You find double negatives.* Double negatives are taboo in writing. They destroy clarity. Consider the following sentence:

The study on global warming suggests it would not be unthinkable that the polar ice caps would be gone in twenty years.

"It would not be unthinkable" is a double-negative. The clause contains both "not" and "un-." As in mathematics, one negative cancels the other. So this sentence is saying that the possibility that the ice caps would disappear is something to think about. However, the double negative requires the reader to puzzle out that meaning. That may or may not be what the writer meant to say, and the reader may or may not interpret it that way. It is far better to avoid the double negative and ensure understanding by editing the sentence to make it more straightforward:

> The study on global warming suggests that the polar ice caps will be gone in twenty years.

Not only is the meaning clearer, but the edit prevents the extra words from cluttering the sentence.

■ *You find awkward or meaningless phrases.* Long or unnecessary introductory phrases that often begin with, "As …" or, "Being that …" tend to obscure meaning. They complicate the sentence structure and often result in grammatical errors. The sentence below, for instance, was written for a paper about the psychological implications of music. The introductory phrase contains grammatical errors that focus the audience on the essay, rather than on the point the student wanted to make.

> As the reader, understanding Smith's essay that music has enormous impact in one's life is very important.

Without worrying too much about the grammatical rules that should apply, it is easy to see that the sentence can be fixed by simply making a straightforward statement.

Smith's essay points out the enormous impact of music on everyday life.

■ *You overused the passive voice.* Verbs indicate actions that a subject performs (active voice) or actions that are performed on the subject (passive voice). Passive voice has a more formal tone, but it can also cloud meaning by calling more attention to the tone than to the meaning of the sentence. Let the action carry the sentence, and do not rely heavily on passive voice; instructors often discourage its use. In editing, watch for opportunities to use active verbs that put the action at the beginning of your sentences and reveal where the discussion is headed. Note the difference between these sentences:

Passive: Consistent leadership is needed through times of war and economic hardship.

Active: The country needs consistent leadership through times of war and economic hardship.

Words

It is generally good to avoid jargon and slang, but a funny thing about both is that they sometimes enter the language in respectable ways to become part of the general lexicon. Quite a number of expressions referring to computers and the Internet, for instance, have evolved from the realm of jargon to become terms we use every day. Words like microprocessor, Wi-Fi, and even acronyms such RAM, VCR, DVD, and IM have entered the general language. So have words like spam, virus, and worms that have traditional definitions meaning something far different from their application in the computer world. Consider your audience when using these words and ask yourself if your meaning will be perfectly clear. Be sure that the context establishes how they are being used.

Use a thesaurus to find new words that approximate the word you want to replace. Then use your dictionary to be sure the new word means precisely what you want to say. The dictionary will show you just how close it gets. Dictionaries follow very specific formats and provide much more information about the word than just a definition. They are designed to help you understand the history of the word, how it is structured and applied in a sentence, and, very often, give you sentences to show you how they are used.

The dictionary also provides phonetic spellings to show you how to pronounce the word and will tell you what part of speech it is—a noun (n), verb (v), adverb (adv.), or adjective (adj.).

Almost all pocket dictionaries include these basic features. Bigger, more comprehensive desk dictionaries can include much more, such as the entomology, or the history of the word and its original meaning. And frequently, they will show how to correctly use the word in a sentence.

Chapter 7

Preparing Your Submission

Before submitting your paper, it is always advisable to give it one last look. Use the tools that are available to you, including the spell-checker and grammar checker. However, remember that these are no substitute for careful checking and revision on your part. Spell-checkers and grammar checkers cannot detect many of the problems in sentence structure and word use that come up in student writing. Spell-checkers cannot detect usage; they check only for correct spellings. A spell-checker would find nothing wrong in the following sentence:

> They published the results of there experiments in *the American Journal of Science.*

It does not know that you need a possessive in front of "experiments," not a word indicating place.

Grammar checkers are even more unreliable. The grammar checker, for instance, found nothing wrong with the following "sentence" even though it melds three separate thoughts into a single sentence.

> He had been discriminated against since the age of eighteen when he was qualified to enter the Army Air Corps, he was sent to Kessler Field in Biloxi, Miss.

Pictures/Graphics

There are many ways of communicating ideas, and writing is always the best one. An old saying tells us a picture is worth a thousand words. That is often true. Charts, graphs, drawings, maps, lists, and formulas can be even more effective.

Pictures and illustrations are meaningless if you do not give your readers a context for evaluating the visual information in them. Without a caption to direct their attention to what you want them to see, your illustration may not leave the impression you intended.

How to Include Pictures and Graphics

- Use graphics judiciously to impart information that cannot be easily communicated in words. They should never be used simply to fill space to meet a page requirement. Add your graphics after you have written a paper that meets the page requirement to ensure that your grade will not be diminished.

- Do not copy and paste photos or other graphics from the Internet until you check the Web site's policy regarding the use of its materials. Most include a link with instructions on how to cite and include copyright information.

- Write a meaningful caption that follows an organizing principle to identify the order in which the graphics are presented.

  Example: Figure 1—This World War II map of the Pacific theater indicates the Japanese line of advance in the summer of 1942. (U.S. Army Center of Military History)

- Be sure to follow a consistent format for all the captions. For instance, if you used the example above to indicate a map and the next graphic was a photo, it would be Figure 2.

The Final Checklist

Be sure your completed paper meets the assigned length requirement. Remember, when it comes to completing assignments, "two pages" are not two pages until you fill both of them with text. The number of pages refers to full pages, not fractional pages. If the assigned length is three pages, each page should be filled to the bottom. Many teachers and almost all college professors will not count a final page if it only includes a paragraph or a half-page of text.

Of course, it is difficult to write exactly the number of lines to reach to the bottom of the page. That is not what your teacher wants you to do. The assigned length typically refers to the *minimum* number of pages your teacher requires. So, for instance, a two-and-a-half page paper is ideal for an assignment that requires two pages, and three-and-a-half pages are ideal for a three-page assignment. Take care not to write much more than the assigned length. Submitting four pages for a three-page assignment may be acceptable but six pages, twice the length, probably would not be. Always ask your instructor how much longer a paper is allowed to go. Overly long papers are often a sign that the writer became lazy and did not take the time to edit.

Be sure that each paragraph argues your position in support of your thesis. It is important to incorporate background into your paper. However, the background information that you incorporate must be relevant to your thesis.

Chapter 8

Getting Ready for the Next Time

Learning to write an effective research paper, like learning to perform any other skill well, takes practice. With practice, you will learn which research methodologies work best for you, and you will begin to develop a distinct writing style. Your best friend in helping you through this process is the person who points out your errors and helps you correct them—your teacher. Never throw away a paper with teachers' comments, even if you received a bad grade. Review it and identify ways of doing better the next time.

Interpreting Feedback

The following is a guide to abbreviations often used in commenting on student writing. Refer to this guide as you review your instructor's comments. If you have any questions, talk to your instructor after class or make an appointment with him or her to review your paper. This is only a guide to abbreviations and shorthand referring to common mistakes. Your teacher will likely include other comments on your paper that point out examples of things you did well, as well as problems in the structure and logic of your presentation.

What Teacher Shorthand Means

- SP: Spelling error.

- Usage: The word or phrase is used incorrectly. Check the definition in your dictionary and consider a different word or phrasing.

- RO: Run-on sentence. Correct a run-on sentence with short, clear sentences that contain a single thought.

- Frag or Inc: Fragment or incomplete sentence. Read the sentence to identify what is missing. Then rewrite it with new or additional information.

- CS: Comma splice. This means you ended the sentence with a comma instead of a period. Use a period when the idea comes to a full stop or use a conjunction to connect the two thoughts.

- Awk: This usually indicates a misplaced modifier, or a descriptive phrase that refers to the wrong thing. Keep descriptions close to the things or actions they are describing to avoid the problem.

Keeping a Portfolio

Your best roadmap to better grades or greater recognition on future research papers you will produce is the comments you receive on the ones you have already done. They are your guide to what worked well in the paper and what did not. Red-lined academic papers and negative feedback on professional papers can be painful. It is not easy to be confronted with your mistakes. Often, however, tremendous learning and great improvement comes from recognizing mistakes so that you do not repeat them.

It is useful to keep your papers—and any feedback you received from them in a portfolio. Keeping a portfolio is valuable for a number of reasons.

First, you may have to. Many colleges and universities now require students to keep all their graded work in a portfolio that must be turned in at the end of the semester. Often, your final assignment—or one of your final assignments— involves the portfolio. You do not want to be without it when the time comes. Even if your professor does not require you to keep a portfolio, it is smart to keep one for a number of reasons.

Second, the portfolio shows your progress in the course. This is important because professors often weight the work you do near the end of the term more heavily than the work you do at the beginning. Most teachers look for their students to demonstrate progress in the course. Your portfolio allows you and your teacher to review the progress you made.

The comments your professor makes are your best road-map to a higher grade. With each new assignment, review the comments your teacher made on the last paper you wrote. Better yet, schedule a conference with your instructor to discuss ways to improve your writing.

Appendix A

The Dewey Decimal System

The Dewey Decimal System encompasses 10 general categories of subjects that, in turn, encompass 10 sub-categories. The 10 categories and the subcategories for each are listed below:

000 Generalities

010 Bibliography

020 Library and information sciences

030 General encyclopedic works

040 Unassigned

050 General serials and their indexes

060 General organizations and museology

070 News media, journalism, publishing

080 General collections

090 Manuscripts and rare books

100   Philosophy and psychology
    110 Metaphysics
    120 Epistemology, causation, humankind
    130 Paranormal phenomena
    140 Specific philosophical schools
    150 Psychology
    160 Logic
    170 Ethics (moral philosophy)
    180 Ancient, medieval, Oriental philosophy
    190 Modern Western philosophy

200   Religion
    210 Natural theology
    220 Bible
    230 Christian theology
    240 Christian moral and devotional theology
    250 Christian orders and local churches
    260 Christian social theology
    270 Christian church history
    280 Christian denominations and sects
    290 Other religions and comparative belief systems

300   Social sciences and anthropology
    310 General statistics
    320 Political science
    330 Economics
    340 Law

350 Public administration

360 Social services and associations

370 Education

380 Commerce, communications, transportation

390 Customs, etiquette, folklore

400 Language

410 Linguistics

420 English and Old English

430 Germanic languages, German

440 Romance languages, French

450 Italian, Romanian languages

460 Spanish and Portuguese languages

470 Italic languages, Latin

480 Hellenic languages, Classical Greek

490 Other languages

500 Natural sciences and mathematics

510 Mathematics

520 Astronomy and allied sciences

530 Physics

540 Chemistry and allied sciences

550 Earth sciences

560 Paleontology, paleozoology

570 Life sciences

580 Botanical sciences

590 Zoological sciences

600 Technology and applied sciences

    610 Medical sciences and medicine

    620 Engineering and allied operations

    630 Agriculture

    640 Home economics and family living

    650 Management and auxiliary services

    660 Chemical engineering

    670 Manufacturing

    680 Manufacturing for specific uses

    690 Buildings

700 The arts

    710 Civic and landscape art

    720 Architecture

    730 Plastic arts, sculpture

    740 Drawing and decorative arts

    750 Painting and paintings

    760 Graphic arts, printmaking and prints, postage stamps

    770 Photography and photographs

    780 Music

    790 Recreational and performing arts

800 Literature and rhetoric

    810 American literature

    820 English and Old English literature

    830 Literature of Germanic languages

    840 Literature of Romance languages

850 Italian, Romanian literature

860 Spanish and Portuguese literature

870 Italic literature, Latin

880 Hellenic literatures, Classical Greek

890 Literatures of other languages

900 Geography and history

910 Geography and travel

920 Biography, genealogy, insignia

930 History of the ancient world

940 History of Europe

950 History of Asia, Far East

960 History of Africa

970 History of North America

980 History of South America

990 History of other countries and regions

For more information about the Dewey Decimal Classification system, visit the Dewey Services page at the Online Computer Library Center, Inc. (OCLC) Web site, www.oclc.org/dewey.

Appendix B

The Library of Congress Classification System

The Library of Congress Classification system uses an alphanumeric system to identify book titles. General categories are identified by letters; the categories are divided into subclasses that are predominantly identified by letters. Subclasses are divided into smaller, more distinct categories that are identified primarily by numbers.

The main classes and subclasses of the LCC are:

Class A General Works

Subclass AC Collections. Series. Collected works

Subclass AE Encyclopedias

Subclass AG Dictionaries and other general reference works

Subclass AI Indexes

Subclass AM Museums. Collectors and collecting

Subclass AN Newspapers

Subclass AP Periodicals

Subclass AS Academies and learned societies

Subclass AY Yearbooks. Almanacs. Directories

Subclass AZ History of scholarship and learning. The humanities

Class B Philosophy. Psychology. Religion

Subclass B Philosophy (General)

Subclass BC Logic

Subclass BD Speculative philosophy

Subclass BF Psychology

Subclass BH Aesthetics

Subclass BJ Ethics

Subclass BL Religions. Mythology. Rationalism

Subclass BM Judaism

Subclass BP Islam. Bahaism. Theosophy, etc.

Subclass BQ Buddhism

Subclass BR Christianity

Subclass BS The Bible

Subclass BT Doctrinal Theology

Subclass BV Practical Theology

Subclass BX Christian Denominations

Class C Auxiliary Sciences of History

Subclass C Auxiliary Sciences of History (General)

Subclass CB History of Civilization

Subclass CC Archaeology

Subclass CD Diplomatics. Archives. Seals

Subclass CE Technical Chronology. Calendar

Subclass CJ Numismatics

Subclass CN Inscriptions. Epigraphy

Subclass CR Heraldry

Subclass CS Genealogy

Subclass CT Biography

Class D World History and History of Europe, Asia, Africa, Australia, New Zealand, etc.

Subclass D History (General)

Subclass DA Great Britain

Subclass DAW Central Europe

Subclass DB Austria—Liechtenstein—Hungary—Czechoslovakia

Subclass DC France—Andorra—Monaco

Subclass DD Germany

Subclass DE Greco-Roman World

Subclass DF Greece

Subclass DG Italy—Malta

Subclass DH Low Countries—Benelux Countries

Subclass DJ Netherlands (Holland)

Subclass DJK Eastern Europe (General)

Subclass DK Russia. Soviet Union. Former Soviet Republic—Poland

Subclass DL Northern Europe, Scandinavia

Subclass DP Spain—Portugal

Subclass DQ Switzerland

Subclass DR Balkan Peninsula

Subclass DS Asia

Subclass DT Africa

Subclass DU Oceania (South Seas)

Subclass DX Romanies

Class E History of the Americas

11–143 America

151–904 United States

Class F History of the Americas

1–975 United States local history

1001–1145.2 British America (including Canada) Dutch America

1170 French America

1201–3799 Latin America. Spanish America

Class G Geography Anthropology. Recreation

Subclass G Geography (General). Atlases. Maps

Subclass GA Mathematical geography. Cartography

Subclass GB Physical geography

Subclass GC Oceanography

Subclass GE Environmental Sciences Subclass GF Human ecology. Anthropogeography

Subclass GN Anthropology

Subclass GR Folklore

Subclass GT Manners and customs (General)

Subclass GV Recreation. Leisure

The Library of Congress Classification System

Class H Social sciences

    Subclass H Social sciences (General)

    Subclass HA Statistics

    Subclass HB Economic theory. Demography

    Subclass HC Economic history and conditions

    Subclass HD Industries. Land use. Labor

    Subclass HE Transportation and communications

    Subclass HF Commerce

    Subclass HG Finance

    Subclass HJ Public finance

    Subclass HM Sociology (General)

    Subclass HN Social history and conditions. Social problems. Social reform

    Subclass HQ The family. Marriage. Women

    Subclass HS Societies: secret, benevolent, etc.

    Subclass HT Communities. Classes. Races

    Subclass HV Social pathology. Social and public welfare. Criminology

    Subclass HX Socialism. Communism. Anarchism

Class J Political science

    Subclass J General legislative and executive papers

    Subclass JA Political science (General)

    Subclass JC Political theory

    Subclass JF Political institutions and public administration

Subclass JJ Political institutions and public administration (North America)

Subclass JK Political institutions and public administration (United States)

Subclass JL Political institutions and public administration (Canada, Latin America, etc.)

Subclass JN Political institutions and public administration (Europe)

Subclass JQ Political institutions and public administration (Asia, Africa, Australia, Pacific Area, etc.)

Subclass JS Local government. Municipal government

Subclass JV Colonies and colonization. Emigration and immigration. International migration

Subclass JX International law (Obsolete) See JZ and KZ

Subclass JZ International relations

Class K Law

Subclass K Law in general. Comparative and uniform law. Jurisprudence

Subclass KB Religious law in general. Comparative religious law. Jurisprudence

Subclass KBM Jewish law

Subclass KBP Islamic law

Subclass KBR History of canon law

Subclass KBU Law of the Roman Catholic Church. The Holy. See:

Subclasses KE–DDK United Kingdom and Ireland

Subclass KDZ America, North America

Subclass KE Canada

Subclass KF United States

Subclass KG Latin America—Mexico and Central America—West Indies, Caribbean area

Subclass KH South America

Subclasses KJ–KKZ Europe

Subclasses KL–KWX Asia and Eurasia, Africa, Pacific area, and Antarctica

Subclass KZ Law of nations

Class L Education

Subclass L Education (General)

Subclass LA History of education

Subclass LB Theory and practice of education

Subclass LC Special aspects of education

Subclass LD Individual institutions—United States

Subclass LE Individual institutions—America (except United States)

Subclass LF Individual institutions—Europe

Subclass LG Individual institutions—Asia, Africa, Indian Ocean islands, Australia, New Zealand, Pacific islands

Subclass LH College and school magazines and papers

Subclass LJ Student fraternities and societies, United States

Subclass LT Textbooks

Class M Music and books on music

    Subclass M Music

    Subclass ML Literature on music

    Subclass MT Instruction and study

Class N Fine arts

    Subclass N Visual arts

    Subclass NA Architecture

    Subclass NB Sculpture

    Subclass NC Drawing. Design. Illustration

    Subclass ND Painting

    Subclass NE Print media

    Subclass NK Decorative arts

    Subclass NX Arts in general

Class P Language and literature

    Subclass P Philology. Linguistics

    Subclass PA Greek language and literature. Latin language and literature

    Subclass PB Modern languages. Celtic languages

    Subclass PC Romanic languages

    Subclass PD Germanic languages. Scandinavian languages

    Subclass PE English language

    Subclass PF West Germanic languages

    Subclass PG Slavic languages. Baltic languages. Albanian language

    Subclass PH Uralic languages. Basque language

Subclass PJ Oriental languages and literatures

Subclass PK Indo-Iranian languages and literatures

Subclass PL Languages and literatures of Eastern Asia, Africa, Oceania

Subclass PM Hyperborean, Indian, and artificial languages

Subclass PN Literature (General)

Subclass PQ French literature—Italian literature— Spanish literature—Portuguese literature

Subclass PR English literature

Subclass PS American literature

Subclass PT German literature—Dutch literature— Flemish literature since 1830—Afrikaans literature— Scandinavian literature—Old Norse literature—Old Icelandic and Old Norwegian—Modern Icelandic literature—Faroese literature—Danish literature— Norwegian literature—Swedish literature

Subclass PZ Fiction and juvenile belles lettres

Class Q Science

Subclass Q Science (General)

Subclass QA Mathematics

Subclass QB Astronomy

Subclass QC Physics

Subclass QD Chemistry

Subclass QE Geology

Subclass QH Natural history—Biology

Subclass QK Botany

Subclass QL Zoology

Subclass QM Human anatomy

Subclass QP Physiology

Subclass QR Microbiology

Class R Medicine

Subclass R Medicine (General)

Subclass RA Public aspects of medicine

Subclass RB Pathology

Subclass RC Internal medicine

Subclass RD Surgery

Subclass RE Ophthalmology

Subclass RF Otorhinolaryngology

Subclass RG Gynecology and obstetrics

Subclass RJ Pediatrics

Subclass RK Dentistry

Subclass RL Dermatology

Subclass RM Therapeutics. Pharmacology

Subclass RS Pharmacy and medical material

Subclass RT Nursing

Subclass RV Botanic, Thomsonian, and eclectic medicine

Subclass RX Homeopathy

Subclass RZ Other systems of medicine

Class S Agriculture

Subclass S Agriculture (General)

Subclass SB Plant culture

Subclass SD Forestry

Subclass SF Animal culture

Subclass SH Aquaculture. Fisheries. Angling

Subclass SK Hunting sports

Class T Technology and engineering

Subclass T Technology (General)

Subclass TA Engineering (General). Civil engineering

Subclass TC Hydraulic engineering. Ocean engineering

Subclass TD Environmental technology. Sanitary engineering

Subclass TE Highway engineering. Roads and pavements

Subclass TF Railroad engineering and operation

Subclass TG Bridge engineering

Subclass TH Building construction

Subclass TJ Mechanical engineering and machinery

Subclass TK Electrical engineering. Electronics. Nuclear engineering

Subclass TL Motor vehicles. Aeronautics. Astronautics

Subclass TN Mining engineering. Metallurgy

Subclass TP Chemical technology

Subclass TR Photography

Subclass TS Manufactures

Subclass TT Handicrafts. Arts and crafts

Subclass TX Home economics

Class U Military science

Subclass U Military science (General)

Subclass UA Armies: Organization, distribution, military situation

Subclass UB Military administration

Subclass UC Maintenance and transportation

Subclass UD Infantry

Subclass UE Cavalry. Armor

Subclass UF Artillery

Subclass UG Military engineering. Air forces

Subclass UH Other services

Class V Naval science

Subclass V Naval science (General)

Subclass VA Navies: Organization, distribution, naval situation

Subclass VB Naval administration

Subclass VC Naval maintenances

Subclass VD Naval seamen

Subclass VE Marines

Subclass VF Naval ordnance

Subclass VG Minor services of navies

Subclass VK Navigation. Merchant marine

Subclass VM Naval architecture. Shipbuilding. Marine engineering

Class Z Bibliography and library science, information resources (general)

Subclass Z Books (General). Writing. Paleography. Book industries and trade. Libraries. Bibliography

Subclass ZA Information resources (General)

The Library of Congress Classification System

For more information about the Library of Congress Classification system, visit the Cataloging Distribution Service at the Library of Congress Web site, www.loc.gov/cds/classif.html.

About the Author

Carol Ellison has taught writing at Rutgers University and the New Jersey Institute of Technology. An award-winning technology writer, coauthor of three books, and former newspaper journalist and magazine editor, her reports have appeared in a wide range of publications, including *The Washington Post, The Christian Science Monitor, PC Magazine, Family Fun, Early American Life,* and *Education Week.* She and her husband, Craig Ellison, live and work in northern New Jersey.